M000301175

B-24 LIBERATOR AT WAR

1
With Number 1 feathered and flight surfaces trimmed, *Lady Liberty* passes over an enemy airfield. A survivor of the low-level Ploesti raid, this veteran B-24D (42-72871) served with 389th Bomb Group as HP:T.

B-24 LIBERATOR AT WAR

ROGER A. FREEMAN

Roger M. Clemons
P. O. Box 102
Bartlett, NH 03812

LONDON
IAN ALLAN LTD

Contents

Cover: Three B-24Ds.

Unless otherwise stated all photos are USAAF or USAF.

First published 1983

ISBN 0 7110 1264 4

United States distribution by

Published by Ian Allan Ltd, Shepperton, Surrey; and printed by Ian Allan Printing Ltd at their works at Coombelands in Runnymede, England

Introduction

The theme of *Liberator at War* is evocation: an attempt through reference to the aircraft's peculiar qualities to illuminate the individuality of the type. Contributions from men associated with the Liberator during hostilities are used to further this goal, for in their recollections can be found much that has a direct bearing on the nature of the beast. Additionally, historical high-points and certain aspects of the Liberator's war service that have hitherto received little publicity are investigated.

No attempt has been made to reiterate the complex development story of the B-24 and variants, or to give comprehensive cover of its wide operational use. There are already a number of publications covering these aspects; among them Alan Blue's *The B-24 Liberator* is highly recommended to anyone seeking detailed information on Liberator production or a broad outline of its wartime employment.

The most widely used four-engined aircraft in World War 2, the Liberator served the Allied cause well in a number of roles. It was, without doubt, the most versatile type in their inventory and was to be seen practically the world over in its heyday. The author has many vivid memories of battle-bound B-24s: it was a Liberator that gave him one of his most frightening experiences when, spinning out of the sky burning and abandoned, it seemed set to crash at the spot where he was standing. That it impacted with smoke and flame some distance away is evidenced by this work which is intended as a tribute to a very fine aircraft and the men who flew it.

Acknowledgements

A book of this nature is only possible because of the willingness of many persons to give most generously of their time. I am particularly grateful to James Oughton, the authority on British and Commonwealth use of the Liberator, for providing much advice and material. Also Allan Blue, doyen of Liberator enthusiasts, who once again gave me the benefit of his knowledge. That grand man of US television and radio, Walter Cronkite, gave permission for use of his story of the low-level Ploesti raid, based on an interview with a pilot a few weeks after the event. Special mention must also be made of the Liberator veterans who all went to great lengths to assist me in writing their experiences: Howard Hill, Gp Cpt John Musgrave, Peter Massare, Clinton Roemer and Garner Williams. Also Albert Hamel whose evocative contribution originally appeared in the Liberator Club's Briefing. Other veterans whose help was no less appreciated are Art Cullen, Charles Freudenthal, Edward Hine, William Robertie and John Woolnough. Good friends assisting were John Archer, David Astley, Dick Bagg, Michael Bailey, Bill Bennet, Steve Birdsall, Serge Blandin, Robert Cavanagh, Alan Crouchman, Roy Handforth, Dave Menard, Bernard Mallon, Robert Mikesh, Bruce Robertson, Kenn Rust and Carl and Elizabeth Vincent.

The staffs of the RAF Aerospace Museum (particularly John and Howard Hill), the Imperial War Museum, Public Records Office and Albert F. Simpson Historical Research Center provided facilities and aided research.

On the production side, Jean Freeman typed the MS, John Archer and Ken Ranson checked proofs, Ian Mactaggart provided photographic expertise and Bruce Robertson gave the benefit of his editorial skills.

To all I acknowledge my gratitude and offer sincere thanks.

Roger Freeman
Dedham, England
July 1982

The Nature Of The Beast

Including variants a total of 19,256 Consolidated B-24 Liberators were built; a production figure greater than that of any other Allied heavy bomber during World War 2. Ubiquitous and making a considerable contribution to victory, the Liberator should have emerged from the conflict as one of the most famed of warplanes. Although deserving, it cannot be said to have received that accolade primarily because its activities were eclipsed by the B-17 Flying Fortress promoted by the news media to a point where it symbolised American air power. Men who through long association with the Liberator held it in great esteem could be displeased to the point of anger that the 'Fort' should get the glory when, for them, the 'Lib' was so obviously more worthy. Objective assessment would probably endorse their view, but fame is not necessarily allied to achievement.

Like all major aircraft types, the Liberator was many things to many people. To the aircrew it was a noisy, juddering experience plus the outlook and effort at their individual stations within its fuselage. The mechanic remembered it best for advantageous or difficult jobs of maintenance. For an onlooker the Liberator was a distinctive shape and sound in the heavens. Also, as with other warplanes, familiarity engendered sentiments for this machine inferring a quality akin to a personality, something intangible yet a conviction, particularly to those airmen whose lives had been committed to the fortunes of war with 'the old Lib'.

Physically the Liberator was 15 tons of aluminium, steel and other materials, that through an average 20,000 man-hours was fashioned with some 300,000 parts assembled into a flying machine with potential to deliver four tons of bombs 700 miles from base and return: a 'heavy bomber' of its time. 'Four blunt-faced engines spaced along the front of a narrow tapering wing perched on a long fat body with a bench-like tail at its rear end supporting two large upright tails,' was a contemporary schoolboy view, probably more meaningful to the layman than the formal description of a 'four-engined, shoulder wing monoplane with twin fins and rudders'. This distinctive configuration came

2
XB-24, the prototype, flaunting her flying boat ancestry. The original design study of 1938 resulted from French interests — they foresaw the necessity of attacking the Ploesti oilfields in a future war!

2

3

Sky watcher's view (Observer Corps). 'The classic wing, finely tapered and with beautifully cowled engines so neatly married to it, contrasts sharply with a fuselage and tail that are downright stark. One is left with the impression that the wing was designed first, with skill and care: the project was then beset with a crisis of time which led to appalling utility. Instead of presenting an integral whole the wings of the Liberators appear forever burdened with the fuselage while the tail is a crude afterthought.' *Ford*

4

Tail gunner's view. 'The B-24 has a strange beauty. Through the plexiglass of my turret I watch them for hours. Like shoals of silvery fish they drift up, down and from side to side as the flight attitude of my own ship changes. They look strong, functional and well proportioned. If the designer ever had any doubts I can tell him not to worry; he got it just right.'

from the designers' endeavours to achieve certain requirements expediently, overriding aesthetic considerations.

Consolidated Aircraft Corporation of San Diego, California, were established designers and manufacturers of large flying boats when, during the late 1930s, the threat of a major war in Europe brought foreign interest in their products. As a result of French and British enquiries preliminary design studies for land-based heavy bombers were undertaken. Then, early in 1939, Consolidated was approached by the US Army Air Corps with a request to undertake licence production of the Boeing B-17; this they countered with a proposal to build a new and better bomber of their own design. The Air Corps, showing interest, requested basic layout and date for evaluation to be ready in a matter of days. Thus it is understandable that Consolidated's chief designer, Isaac Laddon, should shorten both design and prototype construction time by utilising the wing, engine arrangement and tail, from their latest flying boat. Even the

4

5

6

7

8

fuselage showed the influence of the Corporation's previous maritime construction.

That the design team would have produced an entirely different layout, had time not been pressing, is doubtful as sketches for a number of landplane proposals made during the preceding year showed shoulder wing configurations. The deep fuselage encompassed a bomb-bay under the wing centre section with a capacity double that of the Boeing B-17. Like a roll-top desk, flexible doors rolled up the fuselage side to open the bomb-bay, then a novel feature which avoided the drag imposed by the hinged shutter-type doors. It was also the largest bomber of its time to feature a tricycle undercarriage, introduced to shorten take-off and landing runs, as well as enhancing control on the ground through aiding pilot visibility. For its day the aircraft was complex with a large amount of cockpit instrumentation and controls and predominantly hydraulic actuating systems. The complexity was to increase with development of the basic design and cockpit check lists for pre and post flight became essential. As such the Liberator would come to be referred to as the progenitor of the modern aeroplane, in that it was flown by the 'book' rather than by 'feel'.

Developed from Consolidated's latest flying-boat, the wing form was nonetheless of advanced design incorporating aerofoil sections, patented by aerodynamicist David Davis, giving remarkable lift performance. This high aspect ratio wing of constant taper offered speed advantages over broader, conventional wings. Compared with its running mate the Liberator's wing area was 1,050sq ft to 1,425 of the similar sized and weighted Fortress. In consequence, the new bomber had what was then considered high wing loading.

Four Pratt & Whitney Twin Wasp engines, rated at 1,200hp each, provided power. These air-cooled radials, proven on other Consolidated aircraft, having two rows of seven cylinders presented a smaller frontal area than the alternative engine, the Wright Cyclone, powering the B-17.

This then was the aircraft offered to the US Army Air Corps and, with modifications, accepted. The prototype, designated XB-24, flew first on 29 December 1939 and subsequently showed a performance and ability more or less as that predicted. Slightly superior in performance over the Boeing B-17, the XB-24 was eventually selected for large scale production as the USAAC's major heavy bomber. The British, already involved in hostilities, adjudging the aircraft promising were particularly impressed with its range. Their orders, in fact, were the first to be filled. Under similar conditions early

9

10

Liberators had a range potential of 200 miles more than the Fortress. With extra fuel cells in the forward bomb-bay range was advanced to 4,000 miles, some 600 miles more than the B-17 with extra tankage. But whereas the Fortress then had no room left for stores, the Liberator still had half its bay empty. Thus for taking a load a long way the Consolidated bomber found much favour, particularly with the British who had a widely dispersed Empire and Commonwealth to defend. While British bombers had the capacity to carry heavier loads, none had the range or speed capability of the Liberator.

Unfortunately, like most American military aircraft of the late 1930s, XB-24 had been designed without full allowance for self-sealing fuel cells, armour and the other paraphernalia that the European beligerents were finding necessary. Moreover, there was no provision for modern defensive armament in the prototype or first production aircraft. The Liberator — a name suggested to the head of Consolidated by his children's British nursemaid — was from the outset in need of much development and with the improved models that followed came weight increases that eventually amounted to an extra five tons unladen, while the gross rose from 23 to as much as 35 tons. There were inherent limitations in the design that were reached and breached with this added weight. As the wing loading rose so did control forces. The high aspect ratio Davis wing, although living up to its promise of lift and speed, brought instability in flight when committed to heavier loadings. From being pleasant to fly, the Liberator became tricky, particularly at high altitude and in unfavourable weather. The Davis wing was also very sensitive to ice formation distorting the aerofoil section causing loss of lift. Unpleasant experiences with Liberators in heavy icing conditions led to the exaggerated pilot quip, 'The Davis wing won't hold enough ice to chill your drink'.

Early in the development programme the nose of the Liberator was extended to allow more crew room in that section as well as to balance the aircraft's centre of gravity when a power turret was installed in the tail. Later additional defensive armament in the rear pushed the centre of gravity back again giving the aircraft a pronounced nose-up

5
Critical point. Laden with presents for the Third Reich, a 30 tons plus B-24J thunders over the boundary fence at Shipdham, England. The nose wheel has already retracted and the mainwheel cycle is under way — on average it took 25 seconds to tuck all away. This photograph also illustrates the limited downwards view from the cockpit side windows. *Henry*, B-24J-155-CO, 44-40279, WQ:K of 44th Bomb Group, was named for the pilot, Capt Pete Henry. *via J. Archer*

6
Critical point. Nose wheel starts to disappear as a 308th Bomb Group B-24D crosses the threshold at Kunming, China. At 56,000lb gross a Liberator required a minimum 1,250-yard long runway to clear 50ft at the end. For higher loadings 1,500 yards was essential and 2,000 yards desirable. *Via M. Bailey*

7
Final approach. The huge main wheels start to lower as B-24J 42-100117, of 392nd Bomb Group lets down over Middle Level Drain at Upwell in the English fens. Unlike other heavy bombers whose main undercarriages retracted backwards or forwards into engine nacelles, the Liberator's swung outwardly up into the wing. The arrangement proved very reliable and was subject to only minor changes throughout production.

8
A giant of its day. A Piper L-4 Grasshopper, jeep and figure contrast in size with a B-24J of 93rd Bomb Group. The L-4 is standing clear of the bomber's wing. B-24 tail fins were 12ft high.

9
With maximum war load and ball turret extended the B-24H and J models became progressively more unstable as altitude increased over 30,000ft. In adverse flying conditions it was often impossible to operate safely above 25,000ft.

10
At altitudes above 21,000ft B-24 formations tended to be loose, stability problems making it desirable that aircraft did not fly too close and risk collision. These 466th Bomb Group Liberators en route to a target are led by a pathfinder with H2X radome lowered. All other aircraft have Carpet-Blinker sets (the antenna enclosed in plastic 'bumps' under forward fuselage) for jamming the flak batteries' gun-laying radar. *via J. Woolnough*

11

11
In the denser air at lower altitudes B-24 formations were as regular and tightly spaced as those of B-17s. The B-24 crews claimed more so, and the concentration of their bomb patterns appeared to justify this. The 467th Bomb Group, depicted, claimed a European theatre record when a whole formation placed all bombs within 500ft of the aiming point.

12
Touch me there and I'll scream! A 491st Bomb Group gunner keep a watchful eye on another Liberator flying very close formation — especially as the guy in the pilot's seat is wielding a camera. *via T. Parker*

13
Result of a heavy crash-landing; the fuselage crumpled under the weight of wings, fuel and engines. This 389th Bomb Group B-24L suffered power failure after take-off and came down at Fundenhall, England.
via M. Bailey

13

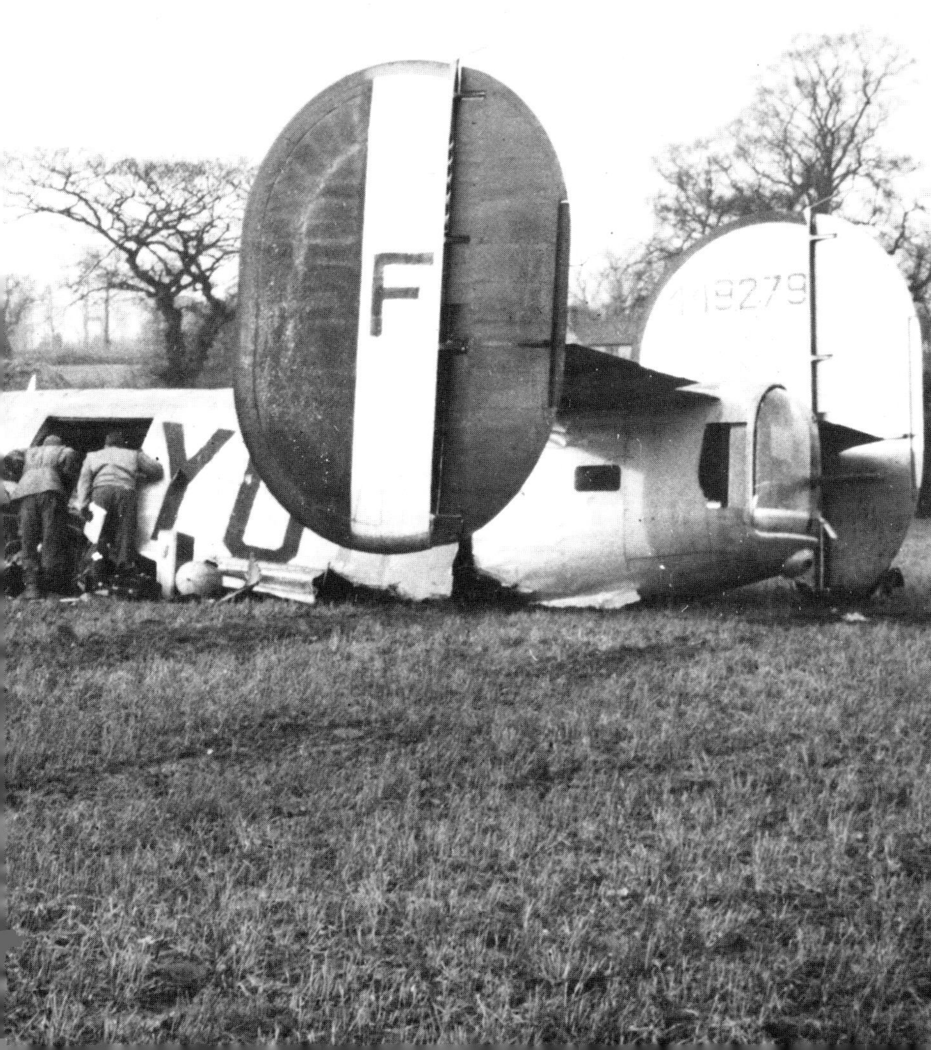

stance in level flight restricting the already poor downward view from the cockpit. The installation of a heavy nose turret that followed should have helped counter the centre of gravity shift, but by then an overall increase in gross weight had so reduced speed and climb that directional stability was affected. The nose turret further restricted the view over the nose from the cockpit and obstructed the outlook of both bombardier and navigator. Moreover, the increases in weight meant that in operational theatres, particularly those where the Liberator was used for high altitude bombing, more fuel had to be carried to compensate for loss of performance and to allow for this extra weight the bomb load was correspondingly reduced. Eventually a point was reached where in such operational conditions the Liberator's abilities fell below that of the Fortress. Only by shedding rear armament and other war trappings was directional stability and performance restored. These were serious difficulties for the USAAF in Europe to resolve, but less pressing in warmer theatres where the Liberator worked at lower altitudes.

In common with its contemporaries the Liberator's design to meet air warfare requirements had seemingly little regard for crew or even aircraft survival in battle or emergency situations. With high wing loading and poor flight characteristics, the Liberator could rarely survive heavy damage to flying surfaces. The fact that some did return with heavy damage to wing and empennage was largely due to the extraordinary skill of the pilots. The location of the main fuel tanks in the centre section of the shoulder wing, and a troublesome fuel transfer system, constituted a fire hazard. Fuel seeping from tanks and connections, drained down the wing and into the bomb-bay. Additionally, in manipulating the transfer system — fitted to the forward bomb-bay bulkhead — fuel often seeped from connections. Thus at times the bomb-bay harboured petrol fumes; although partly dissipated by draughts during flight, the incendiary potential remained and was occasionally fatal! It became general practice to keep bomb doors partly open when the aircraft was parked or taxiing to avoid a build-up of fumes, which might be ignited by a spark from the electricity driven hydraulic pump situated in the bay.

By the shoulder wing configuration, the weight of the wing, with its engines and fuel tanks pressed down upon the fuselage. In a heavy crash-landing the fuselage crumpled under the weight, crushing those beneath. Crew casualties in such crashes were much higher than in aircraft with low-set wings to absorb much of the shock, although overall the Liberator's accident rate was not appreciably greater than the Fortress. In the continental United States the accident rate for USAAF B-24s was 35% 100,000 flying hours to 30% for the B-17s. However, the casualty rate for B-24s in these accidents was almost double that for B-17s, while fatalities were approximately five B-24 men killed for every three B-17 men. In operational theatres a similar pattern existed. During the last winter of the war five B-24s crashed for every three B-17s with the 8th Air Force in England, again reflecting the handling difficulties of the former. Many fatalities were attributed to the inability of crewmen to make quick egress from the Liberator, the location of escape hatches in relation to crew positions being decidedly poor.

There is a certain irony in the fact that the Liberator, product of a manufacturer distinguished in the field of flying-boats, was a veritable death trap if put down on water. The occasions where all crew members escaped a ditching were rare for usually the bomb-bay doors collapsed on impact, flooding and breaking the aircraft allowing little chance of getting out.

In one respect or another every warplane exhibited design deficiencies and the Liberator suffered less than some of its contemporaries. For the majority of its aircrew, many of whom never had an opportunity to compare the Liberator with other big aircraft, its worth and worthiness were unquestioned. Unaware of the inherent design weakness that might lessen their chances of survival, they did their job as directed and, as records show, to great effect. For the individual who knew or flew the giant, opinion was shaped by experience. Some feared and found no favour; others were loyal and laudatory. Whatever individual opinions were held, no one was indifferent to the Liberator. While acknowledging that beauty is in the eye of the beholder, the 'Lib' was not generally viewed as a pretty aeroplane. Heavy featured and flaunting its flying-boat ancestry, it received only uncomplimentary appellations. Accomplishment was another matter. The Liberator shouldered the major share of America's bombing and maritime reconnaissance effort and a goodly part of that for British Commonwealth nations. It also carried the day for long-range air transport when no other suitable aircraft were available. Overall a redoubtable warplane that performed its mission well.

14

14
A wise precaution on parking a Liberator was the placement of a block under the rear fuselage bumper skid. Failure to do this could lead to the nose coming off the ground in the event of weighty servicing activities on the tail end. This 490th Bomb Group B-24H has had the rubber de-icer boots removed from the fin leading edges. The boots were considered a hazard in combat as if lacerated they could jam control surfaces.

15

15
It was said that in battle the B-24 was more vulnerable than the B-17. Sights such as this lent force to the assertion. Victims of a flak barrage, two Liberators slide away from the 460th Bomb Group formation. One has its main fuel tanks ablaze, the other a fire in the left wing. *IWM*

Where, When And Why

Selected for mass production and eventually assembled by five separate plants in the United States, the supply of Liberators did not meet the demand until the winter of 1943-44. But the following spring, with production running close to a thousand B-24s a month, requirements were more than satisfied. As a result, B-24 plants operated by Douglas at Tulsa in Oklahoma, North American at Dallas and Consolidated at Fort Worth in Texas went over to other projects by 1945. The two remaining sources, the giant Ford plant at Willow Run, Michigan and the original Consolidated factory at San Diego, together turning out over 400 B-24s a month, were more than sufficient to allow for attrition. Of the 19,256 Liberators and variants built, 15,070 went to the USAAF, 1,741 to the US Navy and the remaining 2,445 to British and Commonwealth air forces. However, wastage was such that at any one time there was never more than 7,700 Liberators on charge, this peak being in the autumn of 1944 when the USAAF had 6,000, the US Navy 650 and other air forces 1,050.

Figures of the total number of Liberators on charge are not a true guide to their operational effectiveness, this is judged by the number deployed in operational units. To support these, many Liberators were in conversion or training units, while others were in depots for modification or repair. Operational deployment was usually by squadrons, the basic operational unit in most air forces including the RAF, RAAF, RCAF, SAAF and USN; but in the USAAF the group, comprising four squadrons, was usually the basic unit. The establishment of an RAF squadron was 16 Liberators and remained so until near the end of the war when some special squadrons had an increase to 24. The US Navy complement was 13 for a patrol bomber squadron and eight for one with a photographic mission. USAAF heavy bomber squadron establishment, originally eight, was raised to nine later in 1942 and 14 in the autumn of 1943 and a year later, with the addition of four spares, this increased to 18. However in practice, from the winter of 1943 to the end of hostilities, USAAF and RAF Liberator squadrons were of comparable strengths.

The first Liberators in service were those used by the RAF with BOAC crews from the spring of 1941, for trans-Atlantic transportation of personnel. Later that year the USAAF equivalent to these early RAF Mk Is, was the B-24A also used for long range communications transport. In June 1941 the RAF formed the first Liberator squadron with a few Mk Is for anti-submarine duties with Coastal Command over the north Atlantic. The Liberator II was an exclusively British order, but the USAAF made use of many that were undelivered when America became involved in hostilities from 7 December 1941. That month a few Liberator IIs reached the RAF

16

16
Ailsa Craig was a familiar checkpoint near the end of the trans-Atlantic route to Prestwick Scotland. AL627 of the Return Ferry Service served on this run for over four years flying 5,004 hours. One of the Liberator IIs commandeered by the USAAF soon after America came into the war, it was returned to the British in May 1942. *IWM*

in Egypt and the majority of those reaching the UK for the RAF were sent on to the Middle East in the spring of 1942 to form a bombing squadron. USAAF Liberator IIs, known in that service by the manufacturer's design proposal designation LB-30, were hurriedly despatched to Java as part of the abortive effort to stem the Japanese offensive in that area. A few surviving moved on to India where, in the spring of 1942, they were reinforced by some of the first B-24D models then becoming available. Other LB-30s served as long-range transports and communications aircraft in the Pacific war zones, while a few were impressed for oceanic patrol around the Panama canal.

Initially the deployment of the B-24D, the first combat-worthy production Liberator featuring turbo-supercharged engines and power-operated gun turrets, tended to be dictated by the vicissitudes of war. A provisional unit formed with 23 B-24Ds for a flag waving raid on Japan was detained in the Middle East while en route to China and remained, later to become the nucleus of a four squadron group. Japanese landings in the Aleutian Islands, threatening Alaska, created an emergency bringing enough Liberators to the area to form a squadron, which was joined by another from the B-24 training grounds the following month. The first trained B-24D group sent overseas went to the Middle East in July, where the war situation was still critical, engaging in day bombing with the detained US B-24 unit mentioned, chiefly against Axis supply bases, while the RAF Liberators operated at night. The next two new groups went to the United Kingdom, for which the majority of US heavy bomber units were scheduled to form a strategic bombing force for attacks on German industry. However, such was the perilous situation confronting Australia that the next B-24D group was sent there. Indeed, the Pacific theatres of war were the recipients of all new Liberator units during the next seven months as the B-24 was the only heavy bomber possessing the long range so essential to conducting operations in these vast battle areas. Then the demand for Liberators in maritime reconnaissance and anti-submarine work, for which both the US Navy and RAF were pressing, delayed the formation of more USAAF bombing units.

Build-up of USAAF B-24 forces in the war against Germany, which had priority in the Allied cause, did not really get underway until the autumn of 1943 and was not completed until the following May. The biggest contingent, in fact the largest of all Liberator forces, was that of the 8th Air Force in the United Kingdom which had 1,600 Liberators in 79 squadrons at peak inventory during midsummer 1944. Of these, 74 squadrons

17

18

19

20

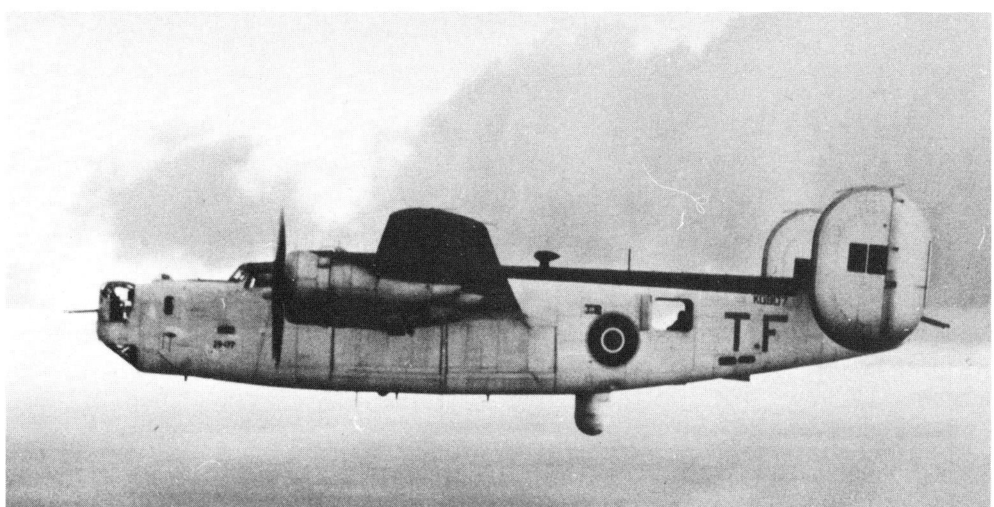

17
Although a high altitude bomber, the Liberator was occasionally called upon to fly very low in very hostile environments. These two aircraft of 93rd Bomb Group passing over a British tank column were engaged in dropping supplies to Allied airborne troops during the crossing of the Rhine on 24 March 1945. During this and similar missions the large slow bombers suffered heavy loss and damage from ground fire.

18
The 8th Air Force's most unfortunate bomber group was the 492nd which lost 57 Liberators in 64 missions. This one, B-24J 44-40161, went down on 20 June 1944 on its 21st mission.

19
At the end of World War 2 the largest force of Liberator bombers was with the 15th Air Force in Italy. This example, displaying the colourful yellow and black tail markings and cougar nose insignia of 460th Bomb Group, strains to maintain altitude in characteristic nose-up attitude. Waist gunners in this aircraft have the benefit of glazed waist windows to keep out slipstream blast. *via W. Larkins*

20
The Liberator became the principal RAF maritime reconnaissance aircraft in both Atlantic and Indian Ocean areas. This Liberator GR VI, KG907 of 1674 HCU, has its centrimetric radar antenna lowered to scan the ocean for shipping. The 'Lib' was the top U-boat killer.
via M. Bailey

were operating in a daylight strategic bombing role, four in night supply drops to resistance organisations in occupied territories, and one in long-range weather reconnaissance. Twenty of the bombing squadrons converted to B-17s in the late summer and autumn of 1944 in a move to standardise equipment in one air division. During this period another four bombing squadrons were disbanded and a squadron engaged in dropping propaganda leaflets at night over enemy territory, plus another specialising in radio counter-measures, changed from B-17s to B-24s. There were also approximately a hundred B-24s in the UK at this time engaged in training and transportation duties, the latter including some modified to carry 4,850gal of fuel and designated C-109s. Used by the 9th Air Force they flew tanker deliveries from England to liberated territory on the Continent, some 30 being distributed among a number of troop-carrier and transport squadrons. A very limited use of Liberators in the UK was in the 'Aphrodite' project where war-weary examples were filled with high explosive and radio-control equipment for guidance to a target as a form of flying bomb. Only two such launches were made, involving a B-24D and a PB4Y-1. The sole RAF Bomber Command squadron with Liberators was employed in radio counter-measures in support of the night bombing offensive.

The second largest assembly of B-24 units was with the US 15th Air Force in Italy, where the eight squadrons forming the US Middle East heavy bomber force had moved in November 1943 to be joined by another 52 squadrons from the United States. The 15th, whose full complement of B-24 units was achieved in May 1944, conducted daylight operations against targets in northern Italy, southern Germany and the Balkans. Additionally a single B-24 squadron operated in a clandestine supply role over the Balkans and in the last few months of hostilities was joined by a similar squadron from the UK. Fifteenth Air Force Liberator numbers were about equal to that of the 8th Air Force during the last four months of hostilities with an average of just over 1,000 aircraft. The RAF's original Liberator bomber squadron established in the Middle East in June 1942 also moved into Italy where the conversion of four other RAF and

21

22

21
First US anti-U-boat Liberators operating in the western Atlantic were those of 479th Antisubmarine Group based in Devon, England, and 480th Antisubmarine Group in French Morocco. They operated for four months during the summer of 1943 and were then disbanded. This tail-heavy radar-equipped B-24D (42-63773) served with 479th Group. *G. Weckbacker*

22
The US Navy participated in the anti-submarine campaign in the Atlantic and from the spring of 1943 had Liberator units working with RAF Coastal Command. PB4Y-1, S for Sugar, of VB-105 is seen returning from a patrol over the Bay of Biscay in December 1943. Sea-scanning radome is extended.

23
Up in the Aleutian Islands a tiny force of Liberators kept a watchful eye on Japanese activities in the northern Pacific and made occasional stabs at enemy bases in the Kurile Islands. B-24D, 41-23884, of 404th Bomb Squadron, 28th Composite Group survived a disastrous mission to Paramushiro on 11 September 1943 when three of seven bombers sent were lost. Note sea scanning radar aerials along spine of rear fuselage. *IWM*

24
The 11th Bomb Group played a prominent part in bombing Japanese islands bases across the Central Pacific. Here a 431st Bomb Squadron B-24J that had at this time, June 1944, participated in 34 of these and claimed two enemy fighters, circles its base on the coral sliver known as Kwajalein in the Marshall Islands. *via M. Bailey*

two SAAF squadrons during the latter half of 1944 and early 1945 made a sizeable night bombing force. These units operated in the same general area as the 15th Air Force but performed specialised tasks such as mining the Danube and supply dropping in addition to night bombing. Two other RAF squadrons in Italy used a few Liberators for long range supply drops during this period. In March 1945 the Italian-based RAF and SAAF Liberator strength was some 100 aircraft.

Other Liberator squadrons in the war against Germany were those of the US Navy, RAF Coastal Command, the RCAF Eastern Air Command engaged in maritime reconnaissance and anti-submarine work. On the eastern side of the Atlantic RAF units predominated in this role. Although the first Liberator squadron was formed in 1941 it was not until early in 1943 that sufficient aircraft were available to fully equip another. By mid-1944 there were eight squadrons using bases in Iceland, Scotland and Northern Ireland plus one at Dakar, West Africa and another in the Azores. Coastal Command Liberator squadrons, with an authorised strength of 16 aircraft were often moved from one base area to another as U-boat activity or Allied naval operations demanded. The American contribution to the war against the U-boat in the eastern Atlantic originated with two squadrons of B-24Ds that began flying from French Morocco in June 1943 and four squadrons in western England which joined them the following month in patrols over the Bay of Biscay and adjacent Atlantic areas. Their existence was short-lived as in October 1943 all maritime reconnaissance was taken over by the US Navy. US Navy PB4Y-1 squadrons began work from both Iceland and French Morocco in April 1943, those in Iceland moving to western England in August where, eventually, five such units were based. In October 1943 another PB4Y-1 squadron began operations over the south Atlantic from Ascension Island. Like RAF Coastal Command, with whom they co-operated, US Navy Liberator squadrons shifted locations and at maximum strength there were eight such patrol bomber units covering areas of the Atlantic with some 100 aircraft available.

On the western side of the Atlantic the RCAF's first Liberator squadron was formed in April 1943 and flew anti-submarine patrols from Newfoundland. A second RCAF squadron became operational in August 1944 and covered the same north-west Atlantic area. US Navy PB4Y-1 units covered the western Atlantic from airfields in the eastern US and the Caribbean although as a home station area units withdrawn from operational tours were usually involved.

In the war with Japan the Liberator ultimately reigned as the only heavy bomber type in six of the seven numbered US Air Forces, and in the seventh it served in a reconnaissance role. During the latter part of 1942 the first steps were taken in a policy of replacing all B-17 bombers with B-24s because greater endurance was required. By mid-1945 the Allies had 87 squadrons and over 1,650 Liberators and variants, of which the major share was USAAF bombers numbering nearly 1,000 B-24s in 48 squadrons.

In contrast to operations against Germany where B-24 bomber units generally operated in large formations at an optimum 21,000ft on daylight missions, a far more varied and flexible situation existed in the war with Japan. Ground defences and interceptor opposition varied considerably over the vast Pacific and South-East Asia battle area allowing much lower attack altitudes to be flown where enemy forces were weak. A bomber unit might within a brief period engage in daylight formation bombing from 10,000ft, in-trail night bombing and low-level searches for enemy shipping by flights of two aircraft.

23

A single USAAF bomber group of four squadrons operated in China from early 1943 against a wide variety of targets over a 1,000-mile radius, mostly in support of Chinese forces. It had to sustain its own operations by ferrying in fuel and ammunition from India over the eastern Himalayas but was also supported in this work by C-87 and C-109 Liberator variants of USAAF's Air Transport Command. In the spring of 1945 three of the B-24 squadrons moved to India to join the four squadrons which had been operating there since early 1942, chiefly against targets in Burma. From March 1944 a single USAAF photographic reconnaissance squadron operated in the CBI with F-7 Liberators. The largest force of

24

25

25
Against a background of mountainous terrain a black bottomed, shark nosed B-24J-170-CO nicknamed *King's Cross* (which alludes to the glamorous girl with offspring, not the famous British railway station) on its way to attack a supply dump on the Siang River. Assigned to 308th Bomb Group's 375th Bomb Squadron, it was one of the 40 or so Liberator bombers operating from Chinese bases early in 1945. *IWM*

26
Over the Hump. Many C-87 and C-109 (C for Cargo) derivatives of the B-24 were employed on the India-China supply shuttle. With no armament and an approximate six feet square double door loading hatch in the rear fuselage, these aircraft could carry up to five US tons of cargo. Note tripod jack support under rear fuselage, essential when loading or unloading. In the background on this Indian airfield are C-46 and C-47 transports. *IWM*

27
For long range surveillance where enemy fighter interception was a low risk, special Liberators served in the war with Japan. Futuristic shadow trails F-7B, 44-41013 of 20th Combat Mapping Squadron on a take-off run from a Philippines airfield. Outwardly similar to standard B-24Js, these specially modified aircraft had up to eight cameras with six mounted over apertures in the sealed rear bomb-bay.

28
The Royal Australian Air Force made good use of the Liberator during the last year of hostilities. This Mark VIII was formerly B-24M, 44-41977. Engine cowling gills are open for ground operation cooling. In flight at cruising speed their extension could cause tail buffeting. Maximum buffeting occurred when the gills were half open. *Australian Official*

Liberators in the China-Burma-India (CBI) theatre comprised RAF units. From a single bombing squadron brought to India late in 1942 the force grew to 14 by the summer of 1945. Five of these flew in a bombing role, five in maritime reconnaissance — but also engaging in minelaying and other offensive duties — one in supply drops to behind-the-line forces and three in transport, moving military personnel to the war zone. The peak RAF Liberator inventory in the CBI was some 300 aircraft.

South-West Pacific Area (SWPA) was the name given to the war zone to the north-east of Australia covering the then Dutch East Indies, the Philippines and New Guinea. The US 5th Air Force was the major operator and eventually had 17 Liberator squadrons. The four B-24 squadrons that reached Australia in 1942 later moved to New Guinea. Four more squadrons arrived in Australia in May 1943 and for a year and a half operated from the north coast against targets in the Dutch East Indies and Bismarck Archipelago. The 5th Air Force further increased its B-24 complement by converting four New Guinea based squadrons from B-17s during the summer of 1943 and four squadrons previously flying medium bombers in the following January. One of the New Guinea-based squadrons specialised in night low-level radar-aided attacks on Japanese shipping. The remaining Liberator squadron in the 5th Air Force was a photographic reconnaissance unit which began flying the F-7 model on long-range sorties in the spring of 1944. As the Japanese were driven further to the north and west so the 5th's heavy bomber squadrons followed, to the Philippines and finally Okinawa. The US B-24 units in Australia trained Royal Australian Air Force crews to fly the Liberator during 1944 and subsequently seven RAAF squadrons equipped with the type operated in the SWPA most notably in supporting Australian troops to invade Borneo.

The South Pacific war zone embraced the New Hebrides and Solomon Island chains to the east of northern Australia and was the domain of the US 13th Air Force. B-24s were first deployed there in February 1943 to assist in turning Japanese incursions. Initially two squadrons operated from Guadalcanal and were joined by two more in the summer of 1943. A further four arrived in January 1944 to round off a force generally engaged in supporting the Allied counter offensive in the Solomon chain. With the successful completion of that campaign the 13th Air Force moved west into the SWPA for operations over Borneo and adjacent enemy-held territories. Like the 5th, the 13th also had a special squadron equipped for low-level night operations against enemy shipping and this began operations early in 1944.

The Central Pacific theatre of war covered a vast area to the west of Hawaii from whence the US 7th Air Force followed successful campaigns through the Gilbert, Marshall and Mariana Islands. A Liberator bombing force established there in the spring

26

27

28

29
The PB4Y-2 Privateer's fuselage appeared to have a bad case of warts. The many gun positions and antenna housings enhanced the capabilities of this development intended for sea prowling. Because it worked at lower altitudes it did not have turbo-superchargers and was 30mph faster than the PB4Y-1. Privateer squadrons operated against the Japanese during the last seven months of hostilities.
H. G. Martin

30
Liberators also served the enemy, albeit a very few. At least four B-24s are known to have mistakenly landed in German occupied territory and two or three of these were employed by KG 200 for clandestine operations over Allied controlled territory. Claimed to be the last surviving Luftwaffe B-24, the aircraft depicted, KO-XA, made an unsuccessful take-off from a field at Wackersleben on 13 April 1945 and was then deliberately set on fire with a flare pistol. A B-24H, 41-28779, the bomber originally served with 389th Bomb Group and went missing on 20 June 1944.

30

of 1943 was operational with eight squadrons by the autumn. A further four were added in May 1944 when the last B-24 group sent to the Pacific war arrived, although it did not enter combat until November. One group of four squadrons withdrew to Hawaii in March 1945, and the remaining 7th Air Force heavy bombers ended the war in Okinawa.

The 20th Air Force, the very heavy bombing force engaged in strategic attacks on Japan with B-29 Superfortresses had two Liberator units based in the Marianas during 1945. A radar reconnaissance squadron used B-24Js and F-7s to locate radar installations in Japan and the other unit operated in a weather reporting role.

The US Navy also made good use of the Liberator in the war with Japan. First in action, late in 1942, was a Marine squadron with a photographic reconnaissance mission in support of naval operations in the Solomons. Two other US Navy squadrons with camera-equipped Liberators served in the Central and South Pacific during the following year. For oceanic patrol, anti-submarine and anti-shipping work the build-up of PB4Y-1 squadrons at Pacific locations, beginning in 1943, eventually totalled 11. Ever independent, the Navy, in co-operation with the manufacturers, promoted a revised version of the Liberator which was most noticeable for a large single fin and rudder tail assembly replacing the original twin fins. Designated PB4Y-2, the Navy also dis-

31

31
Air mechanics of No 31 Squadron SAAF take a break on the cargo to be made ready for *The Little Queen II*, Liberator B VI, KG967. The South African Air Force Liberator squadrons made a valuable contribution to the night bombing offensive carried out from Italy. *SAAF Official*

tinguished its prodigy with a new name — Privateer. The first units with the type began operations in the Central Pacific area in January 1945, one later moving to the Philippines and the other to the Ryukyu Islands. Another four Privateer squadrons arrived in the SWPA before the end of hostilities, three specialising in the use of guided missiles to attack shipping.

USAAF's Air Transport Command (ATC), known prior to mid-June 1942 as Ferrying Command, used Liberators in a transport role from its earliest days. At first these were an assortment of modified B-24As and LB-30s later supplemented by a few stripped-down B-24Ds. Total numbers in service did not rise above 100 until the production versions for transport use, the C-87, became available in the summer of 1943. These and many later model B-24s converted to passenger transports or flying tankers (C-109s) brought ATC a peak inventory of 300 Liberators in the winter of 1944-45. These aircraft operated world-wide, predominantly in retrieving aircrews delivering new aircraft to combat areas, VIP passenger services, and cargo transport in the CBI. The RAF also made use of the Liberator as a passenger transport with regular traffic from the UK to the Middle East and India, while two RAF and one Canadian squadron plied the North Atlantic route.

Despite the enormous numbers of Liberators serving in combat areas, it is interesting to note that until early 1944 there were always a greater number in the continental United States and throughout that year between 2,000 and 3,000 were always on hand. Many served with training units but during the later part of that year a considerable proportion of the continental United States total were in storage. Within three months of the end of hostilities only 140 remained with the USAAF overseas while 3,500 of those returned to home pastures were already confined to surplus aircraft parks. The Liberator's hey-day was brief.

Very First Of Very Many

Surprisingly, the first belligerent use of the most prolific heavy bomber of World War 2 was as an air-to-air interceptor. This was on 4 October 1941 when Flying Officer T. H. A. Llewellyn and crew flying in the 22nd Liberator built, AM924 'D' of No 120 Squadron RAF on convoy protection patrol some 500 miles west of Ireland, sighted another aeroplane about 2,000 yards away. Llewellyn, recognising it as an FW200 Condor used by the Luftwaffe for reporting shipping to U-boats, gave chase. Both aircraft were about 600ft above the Atlantic. The Liberator began to overhaul the Condor at an estimated 35mph indicated air speed. When closed to 800 yards Llewellyn opened fire with the cluster of four 20mm cannon under the Liberator's forward fuselage, expending 184 rounds. The crew believed some strikes were made on the Condor before its pilot banked the large four-engined bomber to the right into the protection of low cloud. Llewellyn keeping under the cloud was 200ft below the Condor when it emerged. Banking left, Llewellyn afforded the Liberator's rear and right beam gunners the chance to fire bursts from about 600 yards. The Condor dived, levelling out 300ft above the waves and in a further exchange of fire the Liberator received two hits causing minor damage. At this point the Liberator's No 3 engine developed trouble necessitating feathering the propeller, forcing Llewellyn to abandon pursuit. Thus ended the Liberator's first combat.

No 120 Squadron was the first and, for more than a year, the only operational unit in RAF Coastal Command with the Liberator. During this period the Squadron was also the sole provider of vital air support for convoys in mid-Atlantic, the Liberator Mk I being the only aircraft available with sufficient range and endurance; but in other respects they had deficiencies.

Following the prototype, the initial production of Liberators had been for 26 similar airframes in two batches for the US Army Air Corps. The first six, designated YB-24s, were intended for service trials and the following 20 as B-24As for a bombardment group. However a need for self-sealing fuel tanks and armour protection had by then been made clear to the USAAC from their study of the air war in Europe. As the British

32
AM910, LB-30B No 1, the first armed coastal Liberator. The conversion was carried out by Handley-Page at Heston in May and June 1941, followed by a month of tests at Boscombe Down experimental station.
via J. Oughton

33

34

were desperate for any modern warplanes the USAAC decided to forego delivery of these first 26 production bombers from Consolidated and let them become part of British orders for 165 Liberators. So while the USAAC was prepared to wait for their improved B-24 models, incorporating the latest war equipment, the British were pleased to receive the initial production aircraft which they accepted during the first six months of 1941.

The fuel capacity of the Liberator I — as the British designated both batches — was considerable with the wing tanks holding 3,100 US gallons. This gave the aircraft the very long range of some 4,000 miles, far greater than that of any other type in the RAF inventory at that time. Since the installation of self-sealing tanks would entail major engineering work, apart from their greater bulk reducing capacity by some 700 gallons, it was decided to use the Liberator I with the original fuel tanks in roles away from their territory.

There were two particular RAF requirements which the Liberator I would fill well. Many other types of US manufactured aircraft were being ferried in stages across the North Atlantic to the United Kingdom and the ferry pilots had to be returned quickly to North America. The Liberator I could make a fast, direct trans-Atlantic crossing and was ideal for this purpose. The first six were quickly put to work in this way as were three from the second batch of 20. The second requirement was as anti-submarine aircraft to cover convoys through the mid-Atlantic area, currently beyond the range of Coastal Command or Canadian maritime patrol aircraft. A vital task for which puncture of their unprotected fuel tanks by anti-aircraft fire from U-boats was a risk that had to be accepted. Considerable modifications were necessary to equip the aircraft for maritime duties and initially 16 were scheduled to undergo conversion at Scottish Aviation's Prestwick base. For help in locating enemy submarines ASV (Air to Surface Vessel) ocean scanning radar was installed. Additional armament of four 20mm fixed cannon was mounted in a tray situated partly under the sealed forward half of the bomb-bay to suppress anti-aircraft fire from vessels attacked with depth charges, eight of which were accommodated in the rear half of the bomb-bay. For both extra suppressive fire and air defence if enemy aircraft were met, single .30in machine guns could be aimed through rear fuselage side hatches and two more of these weapons were situated in an aperture at the tail end.

To operate these anti-submarine Liberators No 120 Squadron had been specially formed at Nutts Corner, near

33
Plan view of the prototype armed coastal Liberator I, AM910. The cannon bay, ASV radar aerials on nose, wings and fuselage sides, and the position of the retracted main wheels can be clearly seen in this photograph.
via J. Oughton

34
Conversion work in progress at Scottish Aviation Ltd, Prestwick, on two Liberator Is for 120 Squadron. AM928 in foreground has ASV aerials and cannon bay installed. Second aircraft is AM924. The special camouflage scheme was changed when the aircraft were in service.
Scottish Aviation

35
In Coastal Command white, AM916, 'L-Love' of 120 Squadron, looks like a flying porcupine with its array of ASV aerials. This aircraft was eventually broken up for scrap at Baledo Bridge in 1952.
via J. Oughton

35

36
Sqn Ldr Terence Bullock. He flew as a BOAC captain in postwar years. *T. Bullock*

Belfast, Northern Ireland on 2 June 1941. Flying training on four unmodified aircraft began a week later with a small number of USAAF 'advisers' on hand. It was 7 August before the CO, Wg Cdr W. M. Cumming, was able to bring AM928, the first fully modified Liberator for operational use, into Nutts Corner. Others arrived during the following weeks as quickly as Scottish Aviation could prepare them, the delays arising chiefly through difficulties in obtaining certain parts. Due to these hold-ups, the planned complement of Mk Is was never realised.

No 120 Squadron finally despatched its first operational sorties on 30 September 1941 when Flt Lt S. J. Harrison carried out an anti-submarine sweep in AM924 'D', to be followed a little later by Flt Lt T. M. Bullock in AM928 'A' on a similar mission. It was Bullock who, on 22 October 1941 in AM926 'F', made the Squadron's first attack on a U-boat. One of three depth charges dropped was believed to have hit the target but the U-boat was only credited as damaged; indeed, almost a year passed before 120 obtained a confirmed 'kill'. However, Terry Bullock went on to be the 'ace' U-boat killer of Coastal Command with Liberators. Bullock was also at the controls of 'A' during a strike on shipping in the Bay of Biscay on 13 December 1941. Light anti-aircraft fire from naval vessels hit the Liberator and the rear gunner, Sgt Hollies, was wounded by shell splinters in head and face — the unit's and the Liberator's first battle casualty.

In December 1941 the squadron's Liberator Is were supplemented by three Mark IIs and, several months later, some Mk IIIs, but these new models did not initially have the endurance of the Mk Is despite weight reduction programmes whereby all but the most essential equipment was removed. The surviving Mk Is soldiered on until late in 1943 by which time light escort carriers and improved ranged Liberators could cover the infamous mid-Atlantic gap where U-boats had once been able to pick off Allied ships with little fear of aerial interference. For almost two years only the handful of Liberators — there were never more than nine on hand — had been able to patrol this area centred 800 miles from base. Apart from destroying eight and damaging a half dozen U-boats, they caused scores more to abandon their stalking of Allied convoys, saving many ships from being torpedoed. The record of one of these venerable aircraft was particularly outstanding. Its story follows.

Operational Liberator I Aircraft of No 120 Squadron RAF

Con/ No	*British Serial*	*120 Sqn Code*	*Period with Sqn*	*Fate/Remarks*
19	AM928	OH:A	7.8.41-27.5.42	Damaged accident. To spares
15	AM924	OH:D	23.8.41-28.5.42	Missing. 448hr 40min flt time
16	AM925	OH:X	23.8.41-18.2.42	Cr after t/o: 3 k, 5 inj
1	AM910	OH:M	9.41-13.4.42	Damaged accident. To spares
17	AM926	OH:F	13.9.41-10.12.41	Cr transit Flt. Ochil Hills, Alva: 5 k
12	AM921	OH:B	10.10.41-9.1.43	Cr burned Reykjavik. Sank *U-254*
14	AM923	OH:W	12.10.41-12.43	Retired MU storage
8	AM917	OH:F	8.12.41-12.43	Retired MU storage. Sank *U-338*
7	AM916	OH:L	17.12.41-17.9.43	Retired MU storage
10	AM919	OH:P	25.2.42-19.6.43	Damaged. To spares. Sank *U-258*
20	AM929	OH:H	3.8.42-23.12.43	To transport. Cr 9.4.45 Sank 5 U-boats
Used for Training Only				
4	AM913	OH:Z	8.6.41 -17.10.41	To transport. Cr 29.1.43
13	AM922	?	8.6.41-14.8.41	To transport. SOC 6.47
5	AM914	?	9.6.41- 1.11.41	To transport. SOC Canada 1946
2	AM911	?	19.6.41-21.10.41	To transport. Dest 23.5.43

(Abbreviations: Con/No — Constructor's Number. Cr — crashed. Dest — destroyed. inj — injured. k— killed. MU — Maintenance Unit. SOC — Struck off Charge. t/o — take-off.)

AM929 - Queen Of The U-boat Killers

The 27th Liberator built was also the last of the batch of 20 B-24As ordered by the US Army but released to the British. The British designated it Liberator I and assigned the serial number AM929. In Consolidated's books the aircraft was Model LB-30B, number 20. Taken over from the Manufacturer on 26 May 1941 and flown to La Guardia Field, New York, the bomber underwent acceptance tests. AM929 then spent a few days at the USAAF's experimental station at Wright Field, Ohio, before being flown to the British ferrying base at St Hubert near Montreal, Canada. From there, on 20 August 1941, AM929 flew the Atlantic to Ayr, Scotland, transferring to nearby Prestwick next day where Scottish Aviation conducted preliminary theatre modifications — radio and preferred RAF equipment. Nine days after arriving in Britain AM929 was taken to Boscombe Down, home of the Aircraft and Armament Experimental Establishment, where it was used for bombsight and diving trials.

By January 1942 when Scottish Aviation were ready to modify another Liberator I for Coastal Command, AM929 was returned to Prestwick on the 26th. Here the weeks dragged by with frequent hold-ups in the modification work caused by lack of parts. At one point work was halted completely for several weeks while spares were obtained from the United States. Unlike the 10 previous Coastal Command Liberator I conversions, AM929 was fitted with an improved ASV Mk II radar of greater range and did not require the large array of aerial masts. Over six months elapsed before AM929 was ready for operations. Delivery to No 120 Squadron at Ballykelly, Northern Ireland, was finally accomplished on 3 August 1942. AM929 was, in fact, the last of 11 Liberator Is to be modified for No 120, where it received the plane-in-squadron identity letter 'H', and being with a maritime unit was referred to in the feminine gender.

Her first operation was on 9 August with Plt Off A. W. Fraser RAAF and crew, an uneventful 15-hour convoy escort. Sqn Ldr Terry Bullock piloted 'H-How' on her second trip but a fuel leak on No 2 engine caused the flight to be abandoned. Nor was the following sortie, to search for an overdue troop ship, successful as a rough running engine necessitated Flt Lt Desmond Isted orbiting base for 35min until the trouble was sorted out and the mission could go ahead. Then on 17 August came events founding a reputation the aircraft would soon possess for locating U-boats. Again piloted by Flt Lt Isted,

37

37
AM929 photographed on 1 September 1941 while being flown from Boscombe Down where it had been sent for bombsight and diving trials.

38
Another view of AM929 on 1 September 1941. It retains the night bomber camouflage in which it was painted at the San Diego factory.

39
AM929 as 'H-How' and sporting Coastal Command camouflage. Photographed shortly before retirement from 120 Squadron.

38

39

AM929 joined naval vessels in a hunt for an enemy submarine. A suspicious patch of air bubbles received a stick of depth charges although the enemy sustained no more than a good shaking. Two days later Isted and crew, flying her again, saw a surfaced U-boat stalking Convoy SL118. Isted went straight in to attack but the depth charges did not explode sufficiently near to the submarine to cause anything but minor damage. Later on the same patrol another U-boat was seen. As no depth charges remained the vessel was attacked with the fixed cannon which caused it to seek the shelter of the depths. The fact that two U-boats had been forced to submerge, frustrating their attacks on the convoy, was a valuable contribution.

On 6 September, with 10 sorties to her credit, AM929 was sent on detachment to Reykjavik, Iceland, chiefly for use in support of convoys sailing to and from Russia. During patrols her crews sighted three U-boats which all dived before they could be attacked. In the course of convoy cover on 23 September she met an enemy aircraft for the first and last time. A brief exchange of fire took place before the enemy aircraft sought refuge in the clouds. There was no damage to the Liberator and apparently none to the enemy.

After two weeks back at home base in Ulster, she returned for a second detachment at Reykjavik with Plt Off S. E. Esler and crew. Two days later, on 12 October, Sqn Ldr Bullock had her on patrol over Convoy ONS136 to the south-west of Iceland when a wake, seen in the distance, was found to be a fully surfaced U-boat. Bullock brought the Liberator round to attack from the rear and let go a stick of six Torpex depth charges, the third released exploding right against the hull of the submarine. To the astonishment of the rear gunner, who was ready to take photographs of the strike, a large piece of metal flew past his position and the whole submarine appeared to rise in the water before disappearing. Only wreckage and oil remained on the surface as the Liberator

'H-Hows' Victims

40
Pieces of metal fly as a direct hit with a depth charges rends *U-597* on 12 October 1942.

41
A lethal straddle around *U-132* on 5 November 1942. All that is visible of the U-boat is some 17 feet of stern

circled the spot. *U-597* had become the first confirmed U-boat 'kill' for No 120 Squadron, Sqn Ldr Bullock and his aircraft.

Another convoy, SC104, was AM929's charge on her next sortie, 15 October. A radar contact resolved into two surfaced submarines within sight of each other. The pilot decided that AM929 was in a better position to attack the leading U-boat but as Plt Off Esler dived his crew gave the other vessel a burst of cannon fire. The aircraft was still higher than desirable when six depth charges were released at the submarine as it submerged. Although a 70ft wide disturbance of the water was seen some two minutes after the explosions there was no other evidence of success. Fifty-two minutes later Esler and crew were surprised to see a U-boat surface near a marine marker. An attack was immediately launched and the remaining two depth charges dropped but again there was nothing to indicate destruction or damage to the U-boat. No claims were made by Esler's crew and not until after the war was it known that *U-661* and crew were lost as a result of his action that day. Next day with Bullock at the controls 'H-How' completed a hat trick when another U-boat was depth charged. This time the enemy was luckier and escaped destruction. Bullock's crew in AM929 spotted three U-boats on the 28th; one was unsuccessfully attacked and the others managed to submerge before the squadron leader could manoeuvre for a strike. He was more fortunate on 5 November when Convoy SC107 was under repeated assault by a force of U-boats. *U-132* was caught on the surface and bracketed by depth charges; her stern, propellers turning, appeared out of the sea at an angle of 50 degrees before the final plunge. Bullock had his second 'kill' and for 'H' her third. This was an eventful day as two other submarines were seen and harassed during the same sortie.

There followed a series of uneventful patrols for 'H-How' where the crews spent many monotonous hours scanning the seemingly endless ocean. Such sorties were the

42 

43 

42
U-194 is bracketed on 24 June 1943. Some of the crew can be seen on the gun deck.

43
Survivors from *U-194* after 'H-Hows' attack.

norm: sighting and attacking a U-boat was an event. The prime consideration was assisting convoys safely across the Atlantic and Flg Off Fraser and crew (who had taken AM929 on her first sortie) received a signal on congratulation for their part in shepherding HX217 on 7 December. The lone Liberator stayed with the convoy for six hours while some 800 miles from her base. An oil leak requiring the feathering of No 3 engine, terminated a sortie on the 12th and the aircraft had to make an earlier than planned return to Iceland. Two days later the aircraft was involved in yet more action with depth charge drops on U-boats with confirmed damage to one.

The escorts continued during January 1943 and on one, on the 25th, AM929 went back to North America when Plt Off N. E. M. Smith was told to land at Gander, Newfoundland rather than return to Iceland. As the original engines were nearing the recommended time for replacement (600hrs) it was decided that the aircraft should fly to the Canadian maintenance base at Dorval where the engines were replaced and a general inspection carried out. Rejuvenated, 'H-How' was back on the job on 5 April, temporarily operating out of Gander for the following two weeks. Further U-boat sightings were made but either the submarine crash-dived to escape or depth charges failed to release.

A return to Iceland brought nine sorties without sight of the enemy, then on 24 June, AM929 once again made a contact which resulted in the toughest battle of her life. On the way to meet Convoy ONS11, a fully surfaced 740ton U-boat was sighted 75 miles north of the ships. Flt Lt Fraser dived the Liberator to 50ft to attack, shooting with the fixed cannon. The submarine took violent evasive action while its guns opened up on the Liberator, one cannon shell piercing the right side of the nose with the detonation fracturing nose wheel hydraulic lines. Loss of hydraulic pressure caused the bomb-bay doors to creep down so that only two of the four 270lb dept charges released, but the aim was good, the first explosion appearing to be just aft of the conning tower. The U-boat disappeared from sight then some 20 seconds later the bows came out of the waves at a steep angle before disappearing again. Coming round again, Fraser, as yet unaware of the damaged hydraulics, attempted to drop another depth charge only to find it would not release.

The first attack had, however, done the job for a dozen survivors were seen clinging to wreckage where oil and air bubbles came to the surface. AM929 had her fourth U-boat kill (*U-194*) but at this moment troubles of her own. It was soon discovered that in addition to the shell in the nose the aircraft had taken other hits. Another cannon shell had exploded in the outer section of the port wing and machine gun bullets had started a serious leak in the right fuel tank. The flight engineer, Sgt A. E. Parsons, suffered slight wounds from shell fragments in his neck, back and legs. In the circumstances it was obvious that the patrol would have to be abandoned. Fuel was spraying into the bomb-bay from the non-sealing tank but fortunately this ceased once the level of fuel went below the bullet hole. Even so a fire risk remained and the bomb doors were wound up by the mechanical winch and the remaining depth charges jettisoned. The aircraft eventually reached Reykjavik where the undercarriage and flaps were lowered by the emergency systems. Crew members attempted to seal the hydraulic system so that the brakes would function but after struggling for 45min the attempt was abandoned. Fraser decided to land tail down so that the rear fuselage bumper would cause some braking action on the runway. While the flight engineer remained in the cockpit with Fraser, the other five crew members went back into the rear section. Fraser made a slow approach and a perfect three-point touch-down close to the end of the runway, immediately cutting power on the two inboard engines. The outer engines were kept running to prevent any tendency for the aircraft to veer off course, which began to happen after covering 1,000 yards. Fraser opened up the port outer to correct this swing to the left and soon brought 'H-How' to a stop. Apart from a slight buckling of the fuselage underskin no other harm was done. Fraser was awarded a bar to his DFC for his gallantry and airmanship on this sortie.

Repairs took a few weeks and it was 6 August before the pride of No 120 Squadron was back in service. Heavy losses inflicted by Allied aircraft and surface vessels during the spring of 1943 had caused the German Naval Command to withdraw most of its U-boats to the South Atlantic where it was believed Allied anti-submarine forces were less strong. So it was that AM929, in common with her sister Liberators, flew sortie after sortie with no sight of a conning tower or the tell-tale wake of a tracking U-boat. Now too, No 120 Squadron was not alone as many long-ranged British and American Liberator squadrons joined older types in patrolling in Atlantic while light aircraft carriers were also available to help protect the merchant fleets.

Following a sortie when 'H' was fired on by a distant aircraft and replied with 150 rounds at what looked like a Do18, but was apparently a Catalina, the veteran starred yet again in the never ceasing battle with the U-boats. On 17 October at 1820hrs, WO B. W. Turnbull and crew were flying her when a fully surfaced U-boat was seen. While positioned for attack, the crew saw that the U-boat's defences were firing at another Liberator coming in on a reciprocal course. Turnbull opened up with the cannon but abandoned his bombing run, leaving the other Liberator to unload depth charges which fell wide of the target. 'H-How' came in again and dropped a stick of four which straddled the U-boat at about 30° to its track. The other Liberator, a No 59 Squadron aircraft, then made an abortive run followed by another when four depth charges dropped close to the submarine and caused obvious damage. Following close behind 'H' came in again and as a result of a perfect straddle with four 250lb depth charges the bows of *U-540* reared up above the waves and then immediately disappeared leaving 30 members of her crew in the sea. Although this kill was officially credited as shared, it was AM929 that delivered the decisive blow.

This, the famous Liberator's 61st operation, turned out to be her last with No 120 Squadron. Although remaining on squadron strength until mid-December, the improved supply of new model Liberators allowed Coastal Command to retire all the remaining Mk Is that had served so well for so long. The record of AM929 in the war against the U-boats was unsurpassed by any other aircraft of Coastal Command: five sinkings, three claimed damaged and 27 sightings. The grand old lady had flown more than 200,000 miles in her time and some 90% of this total was covered during the course of operations.

On 23 December AM929, as 'H' no more, took off from Reykjavik for Prestwick. Soon No 120 Squadron would have another 'H' with more sophisticated weapons and detection equipment to carry on the battle.

Once more in the hands of Scottish Aviation, AM929 was given an overhaul and facelift. Work was put in hand to convert the aircraft for transport duties. Armament, radar and bomb-bay fittings were removed; a new nose and passenger accommodation fittings were installed. Completed early in April 1944, the rejuvenated AM929 awaited collection by RAF Transport Command and in the meantime served Scottish Aviation on local flights. Transport Command did not officially take her on charge until 8 July and thereafter employed the aircraft for conversion and navigation training. For the next eight months AM929 carried students around the UK. The aircraft was popular with pilots, being lighter and faster than later models. On 16 March 1945 AM929 was despatched across the Atlantic to join No 231 Squadron at Dorval, the unit handling the ferrying of US-built aircraft for Britain. AM929 was to collect and carry pilots for the unit. However, sadly, her days were numbered for a little over three week's after joining the squadron and having logged $203\frac{3}{4}$hrs flight time with it, AM929 was destroyed. Near 5.00pm on 9 April the venerable aircraft was on a routine flight carrying seven crew and 11 passengers when an engine suddenly burst into flames. The fire could not be extinguished and the engine eventually dropped off. The pilot, Captain Glen Voorhees, a former US Navy flier, attempted a crash landing at St Simon near St Hyacinthe, Quebec, but two of the passengers were killed and others, including the pilot, severely injured. In the crash the Liberator brought down some power lines and tragically a man who went to the scene to help was electrocuted.

The value of the service obtained from individual aircraft was never assessed by the British Air Ministry but had such a ledger existed there could have been few, if any, other Royal Air Force Liberators that bettered the record of AM929; queen of the U-boat killers.

Bombing Début

44
Loading AL566, 'P-Peter' for the first ever Liberator bombing operation, 10 January 1942. There was some difficulty in fitting British bombs to American racks, each bomb having to be laboriously winched into position by hand. *G. Challen*

45
Crew of the first Liberator bombing sortie. Left to right: Sgt Morey, navigator; Sgt Roberts, waist gunner; Sgt G. S. Challen, rear gunner; Wg Cdr R. J. Wells, pilot; Unknown, 2nd pilot; and Sgt Sunderland, wireless operator. *G. Challen*

46
Looking back at Ismalia from over the Great Bitter Lake. Rear gunner's view over his twin tripod mounted .30 weapons during AL574's trip to Sumatra. *G. Challen*

The Liberator first went to war as a bomber on the night of 10/11 January 1942. This was Liberator II AL566, 'P' of No 108 Squadron, the first operational RAF bomber unit to receive the type. Wg Cdr R. J. Wells DFC, the CO, was at the controls and the target was Tripoli harbour, a port handling supplies for Rommel's Afrika Korps. However, this first bombing sortie was more in the nature of a test flight to obtain accurate fuel consumption details and to discover any operational snags. The aircraft had taken off from its base at Fayid, Egypt, at 1350hrs GMT to land at LG09, advanced landing strip in Libya, 95 minutes later where it was refuelled and loaded with 12 500lb General Purpose bombs. At 2340hrs the bomber took off for the target, reached at 0445 after battling against a 35mph headwind. Bombing was marred by three hang-ups, subsequently traced to electrical failures in the release systems. No opposition was encountered and AL566 returned to base without further incident after a round trip of 2,240 miles in 10¼hrs at an average speed of 213.5mph. Fuel consumption averaged 154 Imperial gallons per hour with each engine using approximately three pints of oil; a respectable performance for such a long flight. The aircraft had behaved well and this initiation increased 108's enthusiasm for the American heavy. The squadron looked forward to receiving a full complement of Liberators and becoming the first fully operational bomber unit with the type. Fate, however, was ill disposed to the fulfilment of their expectation.

With the imminent delivery of 140 Liberator IIs, in the summer of 1941, the British Air Ministry had planned to employ the majority in a night bombing role, initially in the Middle East to exploit their considerable range. Later, in October, it was proposed to convert an existing Wellington squadron in the Middle East with 16 Liberators ferried direct from the United States across the south Atlantic, while two new squadrons would be raised and trained in the United Kingdom for despatch to the Middle East. Thereafter, as improved Liberator models became available, it was proposed to convert all squadrons of No 1

44

Group, RAF Bomber Command (with bases west of the Wash), for night operations over Germany.

While the United States was still neutral, arrangements had been made for the initial deliveries of Liberators to the Middle East to be made by USAAF Ferrying Command, some of whom would remain with No 108 Squadron personnel for a few weeks to act as instructors. Ferrying began in the latter half of November 1941 only to have the first aircraft, AL569, written off in a night landing at El Obeid airstrip in the Sudan when it ran into a drainage ditch. Salvaging from wrecks was a major factor in sustaining aircraft repairs in the Middle East, and thus conditioned 108's maintenance section were quick to make arrangements for all serviceable parts to be stripped from the crashed Liberator — even though the squadron had yet to receive one of these aircraft! The anticipated event occurred on 29 November when AL577 was brought into Fayid by Major Douglas Cairns. Squadron

46

47
AL574 'O-Orange' at Bangalore, India, 20 January 1942 on route to Sumatra. Note lack of top turret or nose armament. USAAF LB-30 in background.
G. Challen

aircrew were intrigued by the huge four-engine bomber but very concerned that it had no defensive armament or even provision for such. Three more Liberators arrived on 9, 10 and 13 December, also without defensive armament and the second of these, AL566, was immediately despatched to No 107 Maintenance Unit to be fitted with guns and other modifications deemed necessary for operations. Conversion training began early in December and by the middle of the month several pilots had 'gone solo' on the type after only five hours dual instruction. AL566 was returned early in the New Year with two .303in Brownings on flexible mounts in an opening in the rear extremity of the fuselage, an arrangement the men of 108 found wanting. Permission was therefore obtained to try and install a Wellington tail turret in another Liberator.

During the conversion period the Squadron continued flying bombing sorties over the Western Desert in Wellingtons although anticipating its imminent retirement. Unfortunately, further direct Liberator deliveries did not materialise for as a result of Japan's entry into hostilities on 7 December the USAAF quickly appropriated most of the Liberator IIs in the United States — more than half the total production.

It was the war in the Far East that gave RAF Middle East an exceptional opportunity to gauge the capabilities of their new 'American Monster'. The Japanese offensive threatened the Dutch East Indies and among steps taken to meet the emergency an RAF Blenheim squadron was moved from Egypt to Sumatra. On 18 January No 108 Squadron was ordered to make available a Liberator with a crew of five plus four fitters, to carry a quantity of spares to the Far East for the Blenheim unit. Sqn Ldr K. F. Vare took off at 2200hrs in AL574 'O' on the first leg of the trip, Karachi, marking the first time an RAF aircraft had flown non-stop from Egypt to India. The next stage was to Bangalore in southern India followed by an oceanic flight to Palembang 1 on Sumatra where AL574 arrived at 0330hrs 21 January. The return flight commenced at 2350 next day with stops at Madras, Bangalore, Karachi, Habbaniya, to reach Fayid at 1416hrs on the 25th. The 12,000-mile round trip had taken $57\frac{1}{2}$ flying hours at an average speed of 210mph with 150gal/ph fuel consumption. Throughout, the aircraft had behaved perfectly.

Tail guns had been installed in three Liberators by late January and regular night bombing sorties were undertaken, but never with more than two aircraft. On the last day of the month AL530 'Q' undertook its first operation, just having had the Wellington tail turret graft completed. Turret rotation was found to be slower than when in a Wellington, although it was thought that it could be speeded up by fitting a more powerful electric motor. In mid-February daylight sorties were undertaken, long range reconnaissances over the eastern Mediterranean. On the second of these sorties Plt Off McDonald and crew, taking off in darkness, unfortunately throttled back the engines and retracted the undercarriage before the aircraft had gained sufficient airspeed or height. The aircraft wallowed and crashed; the crew were uninjured but the aircraft was in a sorry state.

By March, Wg Cdr Wells had learned that his only prospect of obtaining more Liberators for an early completion to 108's conversion was to collect them from a modification depot in the UK. Official sanction for this was finally obtained and Squadron morale took a lift when on 14 March Wells set out from Fayid in AL577 'N' with a crew and 13 men to ferry back the Liberators. After a stop at an advanced landing ground they took off at 1655 on the 15th for a direct flight to southern England. Nearly 11 hours later an Irish labourer, preparing to leave home for work in Dundalk, saw a large aircraft flying low in a northerly direction. There was a heavy mist at the time and a few minutes later he heard a crash followed by two dull explosions. A party of Irish police and soldiers later located the site in a mountain bog on Slieve na Glogh, a desolate spot. From one of the badly injured survivors it was learned that the Liberator's radio was not working and they were off course and low on fuel searching for an airfield when the crash occurred. The aircraft had failed to clear the mist-shrouded summit of the 1,024ft hill by only 30 feet. Of the 19 men on board 14 were killed and four subsequently died; only Flg Off J. R. Anderson survived comparatively unhurt. The blow to morale at 108 was understandably severe. Wells in particular, a popular and greatly admired commander, was deeply mourned. He had come through 73 operational sorties only to die in this particularly tragic accident.

The Liberator flight of 108, reduced to one airworthy aircraft, was no longer viable in the bombing role. Although AL506 and AL511 with crews arrived from the UK on 18 March, these aircraft had been sent out to participate in specific operations in support of partisans in the Balkans — once again the Liberator being the only suitable aircraft with sufficient range. While remaining part of 108 the whole Liberator flight now shifted to specialised operations as ordered by 242 Wing, while for bombing the Squadron again became fully equipped with Wellingtons. Eventually word filtered through to confirm what had long been rumoured, that no more Liberators would be forthcoming as these were now to be sent to the Far East.

The first of the special sorties to aid Yugoslavia resistance with supplies took place on the night of 26 March and thereafter sorties were flown at frequent intervals. The only deviation came when the success of the German spring offensive in North Africa saw Liberators again detailed to carry out long range bombing raids on Axis ports. On the first of these, 3 May, 108 suffered its first and only Liberator missing in action when AL511 'A', with a crew of five and two observers (one was Gp Capt F. M. V May commanding 242 Wing) failed to return from a raid on Tripoli. The first Liberator to be shot down in the war with Germany fell to an Me110 of I/NJG 2 flown by Hauptmann Harmstorf. Members of this Liberator's crew who were captured insisted they had been flying in a Halifax! On 6 June, AL566, 'Y', carried out a 13hr mission to bomb Taranto naval base in Italy for another Liberator first. Two weeks later the Liberator Flight was transferred and attached to No 159 Squadron, the first fully operational RAF Liberator bomber unit in the Middle East.

48
'O-Orange' at Madras, 23 January 1942, after the flight from Palembang. Some high ranking officers were carried, their identities unknown to the crew. Only defensive armament was two .30 calibre machine guns in the tail position and one .30 through each waist window.
G. Challen

49
Liberators 'O' and 'Q' of 108 Squadron photographed from a Blenheim on 4 February 1942.
G. Challen

The fortunes of No 159 Squadron were, like No 108, shaped by Japan's sudden involvement in the war. Originally Nos 159 and 160 Squadrons were to be formed for service in the Middle East with trained crews produced by the Liberator training unit (subsequently No 1653 Heavy Conversion Unit) established at Polebrook, Northamptonshire, at the end of 1941. At first a dearth of Liberators restricted training and the spread of war in the Far East caused the RAF to revamp the plan for Liberator employment. Both Nos 159 and 160 Squadrons were formed in January 1942, at Molesworth and Thurleigh airfields respectively, not far from the conversion unit to which the selected mechanics travelled daily for instruction in the mysteries of the big Consolidated. Ground contingents of the two squadrons were sent to the port of Liverpool in February and from there sailed for India to await their Liberators and crews; they were to have a very long wait indeed.

As no US-built power turrets were available during the Liberator II production run (July-December 1941) these aircraft were to be fitted with British Boulton Paul tail and dorsal turrets after delivery to the UK. The first aircraft arrived at Scottish Aviation, Prestwick, in November but turret installations and other modifications ran into various snags which, together with the priority of work for Coastal Command, resulted in long delays in forming the air echelons of Nos 159 and 160 Squadrons. The USAAF's impressment of many Liberators impeded trans-Atlantic deliveries and exacerbated the situation. Not until April 1942 were modified aircraft and trained crews available. By then Rommel's rebuff to British forces in Libya, bringing a need for long range bombers to hit his supply ports and depots, had caused the Air Ministry to change the Liberator's bases from the Far to the Middle East. To speed overseas despatch 1445 Flight was established at Lyneham, Wiltshire, tasked to provide a flow of 10 Liberators per month overseas, only to have the first few Liberators and crews of both squadrons temporarily diverted to Northern Ireland to help Coastal Command in convoy protection patrols.

Not until 30 May was Wg Cdr C. G. Skinner, CO of No 159 Squadron, and one of his flight commanders able to leave for the Middle East with the first two Liberators. Rommel's renewed offensive of early June and sweeping advance into Egypt quickly rendered the situation critical and as further Liberators arrived on the scene they were committed piecemeal to night bombing raids. Eleven more Liberators from both squadrons were despatched during June to the Middle East where they were committed to operations as a single unit under 159, an arrangement continuing until mid-September, for only by then had sufficient aircraft and crews to fill the complement of two squadrons (16 each) been despatched by No 1445 Flight. Meanwhile attrition and lack of spares had taken a toll so that the average number of airworthy Liberators in the theatre was less than 20.

When the Middle East situation stabilised, No 159 Squadron aircraft and aircrews could at last move on to India to be reunited with their ground party. On 16 September 1942 when Wg Cdr Skinner departed, the RAF's Middle East Liberator squadron assumed the identity of No 160, with No 159 attached. In the event, only five of the original crews and aircraft of No 159 reached India where, over the next three months, the squadron was gradually reinforced with other Liberator IIs won back from Coastal Command or the USAAF and sent out with new crews from England. Even so, at no time did the total on hand run to double figures. For seven months No 159 carried out long range sorties over Burma until the well-worn Liberator IIs were withdrawn at the end of July 1943 and the unit stood down to convert to the Mark III.

In January 1943 the RAF Middle East Liberator squadron became No 178 Squadron when at long last an air echelon was established with No 160 Squadron's ground party which had been sent to India nearly a year earlier. In fact, the same Liberator IIs and personnel in the Middle East soldiered on simply graced by a new squadron number. The re-established 160 received new Liberator IIIs and crews from the UK plus a completely new mission of maritime strike and reconnaissance from Ceylon. The last bombing sortie by an RAF Liberator II was probably that flown by AL552 'D' of No 178 on the night of 6/7 December 1943. By this date the Liberator was flowing from American factories in ever increasing numbers and the British Commonwealth air forces were able to expand their bombing units with the type in both the Middle and Far East theatres of war.

50

50
Sgt Pat Clarke cleaning the guns of the Boulton & Paul turret on AL552 'D' of No 178 Squadron. This aircraft carried out the last bombing sortie made by a Liberator II. *via J. Oughton*

Long Time Near And Far

John Musgrave

Of the Royal Air Force bomber men who went to war in Liberators few were eventually to have such a long association with the type as John Musgrave. He flew every bomber version in more than three years as a Liberator pilot, during which time he rose from pilot officer to squadron leader. Moreover all his 70 combat sorties were in Liberators. His story is clearly aligned with the history of the Liberator in a bombing role with the RAF:

'My first sight of a Liberator was at No 1653 Conversion Unit, Polebrook on 7 April 1942. I had arrived that day from Whitley OTU where my crew had been specially picked for training on Liberators which we were to take out to the Far East. Pride engendered through this selection was quickly dented as, to my dismay, immediately I got to Polebrook I was informed that sprog pilots straight out of training were not going to be trusted as captains of these sophisticated aeroplanes. The crew was to be split up and I would become second pilot to a veteran from Bomber Command.

'My first impressions of the Liberator were dominated by its enormous size in comparison with any other aircraft I'd seen or flown at that time. It was spacious and comfortable, making British built aircraft seem very spartan. These early Liberators had carpets on the flight deck, moquette seats with ash trays in the arms, and were all very plush. No time was lost in starting conversion and my first flight occurred next day with Squadron Leader Harris, a former Fortress pilot, as my instructor. The cockpit instrumentation was formidable but well laid out. The toe-operated wheel brakes and other innovations were not difficult to master. Possibly the most disconcerting thing was the amount of American terminology around the cockpit — "dump valves", "booster pumps", "manifold pressure", "radio compass" and the like.

'The Liberator was the first four-engined aircraft in the RAF to have a nosewheel undercarriage and this was considered a big advantage, giving pilots a much better view over the nose and in general making it easier to land. Apparently there was some trouble with the nose wheel collapsing on early Liberators and it was standing operational procedure for crew members to evacuate the nose compartment and make the awkward journey back to the flight deck before landing. In my ignorance, on one early flight I went down and stood in the front of the nose taking in the glorious view provided through all that plexiglass and stayed there during our landing. When the captain heard about this he was not very pleased, to put it mildly.

51

51
Sqn Ldr John Musgrave, DSO, Flight Commander 178 Squadron *J. Musgrave*

'The cockpit indicator for the positive locking down of the landing gear was not entirely reliable. A member of the crew always had to make a positive physical check, by crawling into the nose-wheel bay, that the nose wheel was firmly locked before landing. Each pilot also made a visual check from the cockpit that the main wheel on his side of the aircraft was well and truly down. At night this needed co-operation from the wireless operator who shone an Aldis light beam on to the locking mechanism. The cockpit drill used by American pilots for the checking of the main wheels was for the first pilot to call out, "I got a wheel!" and for the co-pilot to reply, "I got a wheel too!" This perfectly logical though slightly dramatic procedure was regarded as highly amusing by RAF crews whose more phlegmatic procedure was usually a curt nod and a thumbs up sign.

'The Pratt & Whitney engines proved to be very trusty which was just as well as the Liberator was very much a "power on" aircraft. When landing you normally did not cut back on the throttles until almost on the ground; there was no floating in. If the critical power settings were respected the Liberator was not difficult to fly and she was a forgiving and tolerant servant. Noise level was not as high as in many other aircraft and I developed the bad habit of often flying without a helmet — or with it half off — finding it more comfortable on long hauls. Communication with the other pilot was by shouting across the flight deck.

'During the first three weeks at the Conversion Unit I ran up 35hrs as second pilot and joined Fl Off Terry Towell's crew. Towell had already completed a tour on Whitley's in Bomber Command and there were three flight sergeants on the crew who also had operational experience. The rest of the crew, three New Zealand air gunners were, like myself, straight out of the training machine. On 29 April we moved to No 1445 (Liberator Handling) Flight at Lyneham for assignment to No 159 Squadron and to pick up our own modified Liberator II in preparation for the ferrying flight to India. After the urgency of our training there followed a boring hiatus as all sorts of problems arose. The first aircraft we had developed major snags and not until mid-June did we finally get on our way, in a second aircraft, making the first stage of our trip on the 22nd/23rd from Hurn to Gibraltar. On arrival a crack in the compass glass was discovered. At that time the American compasses were considered unreliable and thus a British P6-type had been installed in our aircraft, AL564, during modifications in the UK. A replacement was "lifted" from some other RAF aircraft and we then proceeded to swing the compass on the ground holding up the whole of the road traffic between Gibraltar and Spain in the process.

'Departure from Gibraltar was in darkness on the 25th with Landing Ground 224 near Cairo our destination. At dawn we were closing with the coast of North Africa and there before us lay a great mass of desert; brand new scenery for all of us. Our navigation was entirely by dead reckoning but the navigator was sure we were well to the east of Tobruk and far from the enemy front lines. After crossing the coast near Mersa Matruh we went on our way without further incident to land at LG 224. Perhaps we should have realised there was something unusual when the station commander came to meet us. He enquired how we had got on and I brashly informed him there were no problems after firing the identifying colours of the day when we crossed in near Mersa Matruh. It was somewhat cooling to be informed that the Germans were now some 100 miles east of Mersa Matruh at El Alamein, and that we had been merrily firing the colours of the day

52
AL581 'M' was one of the Liberator IIs flown by John Musgrave at 1653 Conversion Unit, Polebrook in April 1942. Ten months later he flew it again when the aircraft turned up in No 159 Squadron in India. *IWM*

53 

54 

53
Flt Sgt Alby Read, RNZAF, working on the four-gun Boulton & Paul dorsal turret of AL564, 'D-Donald' at St Jean.
J. Musgrave

54
Terry Towell (left) and John Musgrave in the cockpit of a Liberator II. *J. Musgrave*

over enemy held territory and were extremely lucky not to have been shot down.

'We discovered that No 159 Squadron was being retained in the Middle East due to the seriousness of the war situation with Rommel's force threatening the Suez Canal. On 26 June we joined the Squadron at Fayid in the Canal Zone and the following night were despatched on our first operation to bomb a tactical target behind the front lines. As Towell opened the throttles for take-off he added a touch of drama to the occasion by announcing over the intercom, "Rommel here we come!" There followed a succession of night trips to pound Tobruk harbour and airfield or the occasional 10-hour round trip to do similar work at Benghazi.

'As the airfields around the Suez Canal were becoming overcrowded as a result of the British withdrawal from the desert, the Squadron moved to St Jean, north of Haifa in Palestine and our crew took AL564 there on 9 July. This Liberator had received the identification letter "D" and became familiarly known as D-Donald. Flt Sgt Bertie Coates, our navigator, being a bit of an artist had painted a large Donald Duck motif on the nose. The only time we did not fly this aircraft on operations was when it was unserviceable. There were the usual problems with obtaining spare parts and as 159's own ground crews had been sent to India a new ground echelon, raised from scratch in the Middle East, had to learn the idiosyncracies of the Liberator as they went along. Most were Australians whose own squadrons were without aircraft. Fortunately, a trained fitter had accompanied each Liberator when it left England so we had a nucleus of trained personnel for each maintenance team.

'Although operations were conducted mostly in darkness there were exceptions; one was a daylight raid on Tobruk to bomb oil storage tanks. Our force was a four-plane formation and we attacked from about 8,000ft and then dived to make our getaway right down on the deck. There was some flak and we had seen fighters taking off while over Tobruk but they never found us, probably because we were low down, just above the desert and going flat out — a good 250mph plus. They possibly thought we would make for the sea. It was a very successful raid as the oil tanks were set on fire. Sqn Ldr Max Boffee, who led the flight, collected a DFC for this job.

'We were very proud of our Liberators. The principal night bomber in the Middle East was the Wellington, compared to which the Lib was very sophisticated and advanced. We generally operated at about 10,000ft, some 4,000ft higher than the Wellingtons. Because there was much more ack-ack at the lower altitudes we were sometimes scorned by the Wimpy crews who said we had life easy. Ack-ack was invariably encountered on our night raids and occasional night fighter attacks were made. In general, however, opposition was probably neither as heavy as during later phases of the war in this theatre, or as intense as experienced in operations over Western Europe. Nevertheless, the Squadron had its losses, and, as ever, it always seemed to be the best who perished.

'I recall vividly one incident, which had nothing to do with operations, but would have served us right if it had ended in disaster. I was doing a hasty air test with an Australian chap, J. S. Tannahill. Immediately after taking off we found that the propellers could not be brought out of fine pitch. We had maximum revs but couldn't gain any altitude and went screaming round the circuit at about 200ft — afterwards people on the ground told us we sounded like 10 Harvards going round. Tannahill was really worried: I wasn't quite so worried as in my ignorance I thought "this is an experienced pilot and he knows what he's doing". He eventually got us down safely and we then discovered that through a faulty cockpit check we had taken-off with all prop safety switches in the off

55
AL548, 'R-Roger' of the combined 159/160 Squadron trundles by. Truly a 160 Squadron aircraft it remained in the Middle East after the departure of 159 Squadron's air echelon and went missing in action on 27 October 1942.
J. Musgrave

position thus preventing the electric pitch control from functioning. A very enlightening experience and I've often pondered upon the outcome had the Liberator had a full load on that occasion.

'On the technical side we probably had more trouble with brakes than anything else. Later marks of Liberator had good brakes, but those on the Mk II proved extremely delicate. The shoes were operated against the drum by hydraulic expander bags which would quickly burn if the brakes were applied for too long or too sharply. On leaving the aircraft one was at once made aware of this failure by the horrible smell it created. It became a matter of shame and disgrace to arrive back in dispersal accompanied by a disgusting smell! The problem was that spare bags were difficult to obtain.

'By September the situation in the Middle East was reckoned to be contained and No 159 Squadron aircraft began to move to their original destination, India. My 16th and final sortie of this period was on 25 September when we parachuted magnetic mines into Tobruk harbour. We started our move on 6 October, via Iraq and Karachi, to our new Indian base at Salbani, about 100 miles west of Calcutta. In addition to the crew of eight, we carried four mechanics, 5,000lb of Liberator spares and, most welcome, long awaited personal mail for people already there. A serious incident occurred when Sqn Ldr Beck, a flight commander, brought another aircraft to India. Arriving over Karachi with a full crew plus several ground men, one of the main undercarriage wheels failed to lower completely. Faced with the dangerous prospect of a very untidy arrival with an unusual number of people on board, Beck wisely baled out everyone except himself and his co-pilot. In the event the landing was made without any disaster occurring — but it was an unexpected way of arriving in India for most of the occupants, especially the ground crew.

'Salbani airfield was still under construction, mostly by direct man and woman power in the form of hundreds of locally engaged native labourers. The place was very primitive with flying occasionally disturbed by such happenings as a herd of cows wandering on the runway.

'First operation against the Japs was an $8\frac{1}{2}$-hr haul to Mingaladon airfield near Rangoon on 17 November where, as there was no opposition, we came down after dropping our bombs and machine gunned the place. That was my last trip with Towell in aircraft "D" — which, incidentally, he later made an excellent job of crash-landing at Salbani when a tyre failed. I was then made a captain and given my own crew. Flt Sgt Wallace, my second pilot, and most of the other crew members had previously been with the two RAF Fortresses that had ended up in India earlier in the year. Usually we flew AL544 "B", one of the original aircraft of No 159 Squadron.

'The rate of operations was frustratingly slow, chiefly due to the usual problems with supplies and spares. As in the Middle East most sorties were in darkness, usually long hauls to the Rangoon area. Navigation was very basic and exacting, nothing but dead reckoning and astro, with only occasional help from the radio. Target identification was entirely by "eye-ball". On one occasion, after some nine hours airborne across the Bay of Bengal and fairly low on fuel, we finally identified, through some murky weather, a coastline. I asked my navigator, Flg Off Bunny Moffat, what he reckoned was our position. He replied laconically that he was reasonably certain that it was some point on the east coast of India! From this wide choice he soon determined from dead reckoning — with no help from the stars

56

above a cloud covered sky, but some intermittent help from a distant ground radio station — a course for our base where we eventually landed very relieved and not a moment too soon.

'We tried to avoid landing away from base at remote airfields unless we had to because of possible difficulties in starting engines. A big drawback with the Liberator II was that considerable external electrical power had to be available to plug into the aircraft's own electrical system for easy starting. This had never been a problem in the UK where a battery trolley with the right connections was to be had at most airfields. But in the Middle East and India such equipment was frequently not available away from base. Later model Liberators had what was called an Auxiliary Power Unit (usually shortened to APU) contained in the aircraft and which was basically a very small capacity two-stoke petrol engine driving an electrical generator. Tucked away under the flight deck it was itself started electrically and kept running for all ground operation of the aircraft's systems and was not usually shut off until all four engines were running and generating electrical power. The APU could also be taken outside the aircraft quite easily and operated externally. APU was American terminology; the RAF generally preferred to stick to their popular name for such a unit — Charhorse. This luxury was not available on the Mk II. While it was possible to start an engine using the aircraft's own storage batteries alone, the power requirement was such that the batteries would usually fade before the engine fired. This method was to be avoided as it tended to cut battery life and, like everything else, batteries were in short supply.

'However, Consolidated had made provision for starting emergencies which was something of a nightmare operation to those who had to carry it out. A long crank handle was inserted into the underside of the accessories compartment on No 1 engine and used to crank up an inertia motor. When sufficient revolutions had been built up in the motor a switch was pressed in the cockpit which engaged this motor to the starter and with luck the engine would turn and catch. It took two men to work the cranking mechanism and it was no mean feat of strength to build up the required inertia motor speed in the heat of India or the Middle East. Sometimes there was an additional complication in that the electrical release to engage inertia and starter motors would not function. Then a fourth person had to be involved; opening a flap on the engine nacelle where a T-handle lever was located and pulling this at the appropriate moment to make a mechanical connection between the two motors. With four people involved, two men sweating like mad on the crank, one in the cockpit and another poised at the T-handle on the nacelle, a tremendous amount of shouting and agreed signs had to be used in performing this operation. Of course, once one engine was running its dynamo would supply enough current to support electrical starting of the other three. Fortunately, it was rarely necessary to start up in this laborious way which must have appeared a comic act to any onlooker. Indeed, it inspired a particular piece of farce which a group of us used to enact on party nights by the bar. Someone would climb up into the roof rafters to represent the man high up in the cockpit, two others would wind away underneath with an imaginary crank while a fourth fellow was near at hand by a beer barrel groping for a T-handle to pull at the right moment. The uninitiated probably wouldn't see anything funny in these antics but to people who at sometime had had to perform this rite it could be hilarious.

56
AL550 'M' served with 159 Squadron in both the Middle and Far East flying nearly 100 sorties. When this photograph was taken in Palestine the aircraft had returned from an operation with flak damage to the right fin.
J. Musgrave

'By April I had completed my 30th sortie and so finished my tour. There followed what was undoubtedly my most frustrating association with a Liberator. The Squadron was asked to send an aircraft back to Britain to pick up a new theatre commander, Sir Richard Peirse. Persistent engine problems led to a grounding when the Liberator reached Iraq, and while the VIP transport job was given to another squadron I had the task of getting the ailing aircraft back to Salbani. The Pratt & Whitney engines usually gave us little trouble but it took several attempts to put this one right including a trip to a Maintenance Unit in the Canal Zone. In all I spent the best part of three months swanning around the Middle East with this wretched aeroplane — AL560. Ironically, when I eventually reached Salbani I found the Squadron was dispensing with Liberator IIs having been stood down to convert to Mk IIIs which were then arriving. The Liberator III was the RAF bomber version of the USAAF B-24D. Most notable improvement was the turbo-blown engines which gave more power and a better altitude performance. The armament was much improved with American power turrets mounting .50in weapons. The first Mk III that I flew was in fact the very first so designated.

'As for the Mk IIs, at the beginning of September these were now placed in a newly established No 1584 Conversion Flight at Salbani which was to act as the theatre operational training unit for Liberators. Having been taken off operations I found myself given the job of acting as an instructor. However, during the first few months of its existence, No 1584 Flight was occasionally called on to supplement No 159 Squadron's operations and flying Mk IIIs I captained a crew on three of these sorties, the last to Mandalay on 21 January 1944. Instructing tended to be a tedious occupation compared with operations and I admit that I tried to liven things up now and then by showing off disgustingly and demonstating to pupils how to *really* fly a Liberator. In retrospect I regret that at times in my callow arrogance I must have treated the ever-forgiving aircraft quite brutally. It was really surprising what you could get away with in such a large aircraft even though you didn't deserve to.

'After a few months I was becoming progressively unhappy about the job I was doing and when, in April 1944, the conversion unit moved to Kola, near Bangalore in southern India, I began making loud noises about being cast away from the rest of the war. Eventually I was given the opportunity of returning to operations but in the Middle East. After a sea journey from India, I went through a Liberator refresher course at No 1675 Conversion Unit which had the Liberator VI, distinguished by nose turrets. Here I picked up a new crew and went to Amendola on the Foggia plain in Italy to join No 178 Squadron. Formed from the Middle East Liberators and crews that did not move on to India at the end of 1942, No 178 had moved in the wake of the victorious armies from Palestine right along the coast of North

57
The demise of AL564 'D-Donald' which suffered undercarriage failure when Flt Lt Terry Towell made a night landing at Salbani on 15 April 1943. *via C. Vincent*

57

58

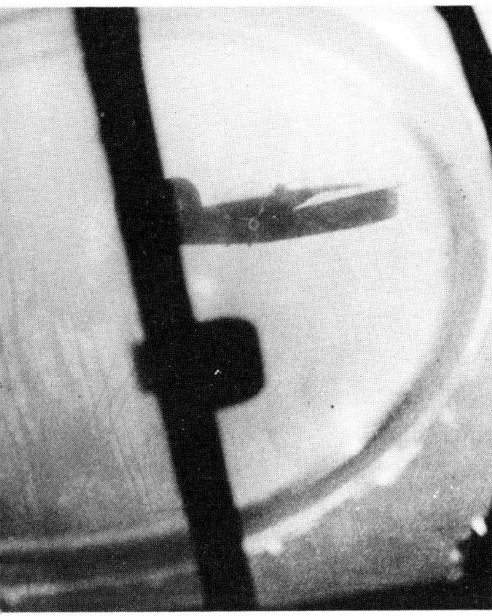

59

58
AL571, 'F' of No 159 Squadron wings over Indian storm clouds in the spring of 1943. Flame dampers have been fitted to engine exhausts for night operations and that on No 4 is visible in this photograph. AL571 was later converted for transport work. *via Carl Vincent*

59
AL544, 'B', viewed through the pilot's window. The 'bubble' on cockpit side windows was introduced on early production of Liberators to improve pilots' outlook. The side windows sloped inwards restricting the elevation of the pilots' positions which could have helped improve visibility. *J. Musgrave*

Africa to Southern Italy. On being driven out to the dispersal area for the first time I was somewhat touched and amazed to discover that the lorry was the same one used for crew transport in Palestine two years previously! Several of the ground crew from the old unit were also still around.

'No 178 was a sadly depleted squadron at that time. During the few weeks prior to my arrival it had flown a number of long range missions to Warsaw in order to drop supplies to partisans aiming to establish a stable Polish government as the Germans withdrew and the Russians advanced. Losses were very heavy and it took some time to rebuild 178 to its normal strength.

'The squadron shared the airfield with No 614 Squadron's Halifaxes, a pathfinder outfit which later converted to Liberators, and four American B-17 squadrons. It was a very busy airfield with over a hundred four-engined bombers using the single pierced steel plank runway. I began flying ops in September 1944, the majority being over northern Italy, Central Europe and the Balkans. Again most work was in darkness and in addition to bombing and mining the Danube we dropped supplies to partisan forces. Some of the latter raids were flown in daylight keeping well away from known German strongholds. On one occasion some poor navigation on our part took us right over a flak battery at low altitude. That we got away with nothing more than a few holes was miraculous. Night fighters in the Balkans were often quite good and accounted for some of the Liberators of our squadron but, although shot at on occasions, we were lucky enough to evade them.

'The Liberator VI was heavier than earlier marks. Electronically controlled turbos and Honeywell automatic pilot were notable improvements. The extra weight of the nose turret actually gave the Liberator a better flight attitude as the Mk II had tended to be tail heavy and have a nose-up stance, especially with a full load. A crew of seven was standard. By this time we had dispensed with second pilots and a flight engineer manned the right hand cockpit seat. They would monitor the instruments and most acquired enough knowledge to supervise flight on automatic pilot and to take over the controls in an emergency. One pitch black night during my early days with 178, No 2 engine suddenly burst into flames after take-off. The engines on the Mk VI had pre-set electrically controlled manifold pressure but on this occasion something went wrong and the engine over boosted without my flight engineer spotting this before a cylinder blew when we were at about 50ft from the ground. It was a dicey situation as we had a full bomb load, but we managed to feather the propellor and climb away. After some anxious moments with a reluctant jettisoning gear we finally managed to get rid of the bombs and returned hastily to base. They never did find the bombs which fell in open country between the airfield and the sea.

'There was one Liberator on the Squadron at that time — EW276 "L" — which developed a reputation as a rogue aircraft. Many pilots were reluctant to fly it because it seemed to develop mechanical failures so regularly. Being a flight commander and feeling I should set an example, I decided to adopt the aircraft as my own and flew it regularly to disprove the reputation. I may have done to others; but I'm not sure that I did to myself. On reflection I don't know whether my bravado was justified for the dangers of the air war were great enough without courting mechanical failure.

'My last and 70th operation was on the night of 22 March 1945 in KH208 to bomb marshalling yards at Villach in Austria. The target was in a valley between very high mountains and these were visible in the moonlight towering above us as we made our run at something over 9,000ft. A Liberator flying close behind ours caught fire and went down — as it happened, the last bomber No 178 Squadron was to lose on operations. The aircraft was hit by an incendiary bomb dropped from another aircraft flying above; a sad final loss for a distinguished squadron.

'Overall the Liberator was a hardy machine with a high level of serviceability and a good operational record. It stood up well to extremes in the climatic and primitive conditions and various roles in which it operated. In my opinion, however, it always had a vague air of being a converted airliner in comparison with such rugged bombing machines as the Lancaster, which I flew in later years. Nevertheless, the Liberator was my life for a long time. She was my first love — and I guess she always will be.'

USAAF Liberator Firsts

The air force, destined to be the major operator of Liberators had only 11 when, on 7 December 1941, the Japanese attack on Pearl Harbor brought the United States into World War 2. Of the 11, two were prototypes and the remainder B-24As, chiefly employed in long-range transport by USAAF's Ferry Command. The total was diminished in the first few hours of hostilities when a B-24A being prepared at Hickham Field, Hawaii, for secret surveillance of Japanese Pacific island bases, was destroyed on the ground. The victim, 40-2371, has the unfortunate position of being the first Liberator destroyed by enemy action.

To meet the crisis situation in South-East Asia, where the Japanese were launching offensives against the Philippine Islands from bases in Indo-China, heavy bombers were urgently needed. A limited number of Boeing B-17s were available but the few B-24As were quite unsuitable for combat as, like the RAF's Liberator Is, they had non-self-sealing fuel tanks. War worthy Liberators with the required refinements and power gun turrets were on the production line at San Diego but the first batch, nine B-24Cs, were basically pre-production models for the following B-24D.

Therefore, to meet the emergency, the US Government took over most of the Liberator IIs that had not yet been delivered to the British. As the USAAF preferred to use a designation rather than a name for aircraft types, the impressed Consolidated bombers were known by the manufacturers' design proposal number, LB-30, there having been no USAAF number for this export model. Fifteen LB-30s were quickly allocated to Project X, a plan to reinforce US forces in the Far East with 80 heavy bombers, the majority being B-17s. As manufactured the LB-30 lacked adequate armament so a crash programme of modification was set up to install a Martin power turret in the dorsal location and twin hand-manipulated .50in guns in the tail. This delayed the assembly of the LB-30 element, formed under Maj Austin Straubel, but such was the urgency of the situation they were despatched singly or in

60
Photographed at Lagos, B-24 40-2370 was used by Maj-Gen George Brett, Chief of the Air Corps for USAAF's first overseas survey flight to the Middle East in September 1941. The pilot was Lt-Col Caleb Haynes and the navigator Maj Curtis LeMay. 40-2370 was destroyed by Japanese air attack on Broome Airfield, Australia, 3 March 1942. *P. Arnold*

60

small numbers as available. Straubel's aircraft and five others took an easterly route via Africa and India, the remaining eight aircraft (one never left the USA) island-hopped the Pacific.

Java, where the Allies were attempting to hold the Japanese thrust into the Netherlands East Indies, was the eventual destination of Project X aircraft. Straubel arrived in AL609 at Malang on 11 January 1942 and on this and the following three days was joined by three more LB-30s. Little time was lost in making use of the arrivals and on the morning of 16 January three LB-30s and two B-17s were despatched on operations. The LB-30s, led by Maj Straubel in AL609, were sent against the enemy airfield at Langoan in north-east Celebes. It was necessary to stage through Kendari in southern Celebes, some 350 miles from Langoan. The Japanese detected the approach of the Liberators and put up interceptors to meet them. The bombers came under persistent fighter attacks and were riddled with small calibre fire. Lt John Dougherty's AL535 was so badly damaged he was forced to crash-land on a small island off the south coast of Borneo where he and his crew (three were wounded) were stranded for eight days until rescued by a flying boat. AL576, piloted by Lt W. E. Bayse, was also badly shot up and made a forced landing at Makassar in south Celebes, damaging it beyond repair. Only Straubel's aircraft returned to Malang in what was the USAAF's first combat bombing operation with Liberators.

In succeeding days further LB-30s arrived in Java, more operations were undertaken and losses suffered. Six weeks later the Allies were being driven out of Java and the LB-30s

61

62

61
RAF ground crew men refuelling LB-30 AL570 at Bangalore, India on 20 January 1942. This was the fifth LB-30 to reach Java and operate with 7th Bomb Group. It was also one of the few to survive the Japanese offensive in the Dutch East Indies.
G. Challen

62
Roamin' Rosie, 41-23698, makes her run on Darwin's sun-baked airstrip and the dust flies. A B-24D of 319th Bomb Squadron, 90th Bomb Group, the first B-24 equipped group to become involved in the war with Japan and flying its initial combat mission on 13 November 1942. Insufficient training contributed to the loss or destruction of seven aircraft on the group's first two bombing operations.
Australian Official

63

were used to evacuate 35 passengers at a time in night flights to Australia. Half the LB-30 force despatched from the United States was destroyed during the Java episode.

The first combat operations by Liberators in the Aleutians, the China-Burma-India theatre, and the Central Pacific also involved LB-30s. In the Aleutians a lone LB-30 was in a mixed force of American bombers attempting to locate and attack a Japanese task force on 4 June 1942. AL608, in which Maj Gen Lewis Bereton departed Java for India in late February 1942, also inaugurated Liberator

64

63
Arkansas Traveler, 41-11616 Halpro No 14, taking off from Fayid. This was the B-24D in which Col Harry Halverson led the first USAAF raid on Europe. *IWM*

64
The ninth B-24D served with 44th Bomb Group at Barksdale, Louisiana training early Liberator crews.

and 10th Air Force operations in the CBI when, piloted by Lt Wade it participated in a night mission in April to Port Blair in the Andaman Islands but was unable to bomb. During the Battle of Midway Maj-Gen Clarence Tinker, commanding the 7th Air Force, flew in AL589 one of four LB-30s, on a night bombing operation against the enemy base at Wake Island. None of the bombers located the target and the General's aircraft failed to return, reportedly having stalled and crashed into the sea.

The first USAAF offensive operation over Europe using Liberators was on a larger scale but equally undistinguished. Carried out on the night of 11-12 June 1942 by B-24Ds of the Halverson Detachment, a provisional unit originally formed to bomb the Japanese homeland from Chinese bases, the target was the Ploesti oilfields in Romania. Led by Col Halverson in 41-11616, 13 bombers were despatched, individually, from Fayid, Egypt and, because of the distance involved, the crews were briefed to land in Iraq on return. In the darkness the target was not located and bombs were scattered on possible targets. Only six B-24Ds landed safely in Iraq and a seventh put down on its belly. Four of the bombers were interned in Turkey and the remaining two landed in Syria.

From Britain, where the major force of Liberator bombers was eventually to be established, the first USAAF offensive operation took place on 9 October 1942 against a steelworks at Lille, France. Led by the CO, Col Edward Timberlake, in 41-23754, 24 B-24s of the 93rd Bomb Group took off; 14 had to turn back for mechanical and other reasons, 10 bombed and nine returned. Under heavy attack by fighters nine of the B-24s received damage, mostly slight, one force-landing at Northolt. The missing Liberator, 41-23678, was shot down near the target.

The combat initiations of USAAF Liberators in various theatres of war had generally little success in their objectives. The crews were in all but a few cases without previous combat experience and with minimum flight time on the Liberator. It took some months to develop the expertise which would eventually make this aircraft a very effective weapon in a number of offensive roles. To utilise the large numbers of B-24s expected when production really began to flow, an extremely extensive training organisation was set up, mostly concentrated under the 2nd Air Force in the north-eastern United States. Initially training was conducted by the 44th Bomb Group at Barksdale Field, Louisiana, in the 3rd Air Force area. The 44th was the USAAF's first all-Liberator group, receiving B-24Cs and early D models although its first Liberator received at the outbreak of hostilities had been an LB-30. Amoeba like, at intervals the 44th separated parts of its complement to form the nucleus of another B-24 group. It formed the 98th Bomb Group, first complete B-24 group sent overseas — to the Middle East in July 1942 — the 93rd Bomb Group sent to England in August 1942 and the 90th Bomb Group which began its journey to Australia in the same month. By then the B-24 training organisation had expanded to a point where the 44th Group itself could be spared for combat and it followed its prodigy, the 93rd, to England.

Pacific Survivor

Clinton Roemer

By the autumn of 1942 the Liberator was the most sought after aircraft being manufactured in the United States: the reason, as always, its endurance. While the USAAF's European theatre had priority and the US Navy and RAF clamoured for Liberators to use on ocean patrol, the most pressing need was in the Pacific war zones where range was a paramount consideration in air attacks to counter Japanese operations. To reach many of the island targets round trips of 2,500 miles were not uncommon. Because of its limited endurance the B-17 was being replaced with B-24s in the war with Japan. The change took many months due to the short supply of Liberators and a high rate of attrition with those received. Committing small numbers to encounter large concentrations of enemy fighters inevitably brought heavy loss. But in these early days accidents took an equal toll among the crews, whose training was inadequate for the harsh operating environment into which they were plunged. The survivors were those who learned quickly how to work with the B-24 in this kind of conflict as related by Clinton Roemer:

'I graduated as a navigator in August 1942 and after a short leave was sent to Ephrata Field, Washington state to join the recently created 307th Bomb Group. Crews were formed — I was placed in that of Lt Stanley Foster — and we started flying in a half-dozen well-worn B-24Ds, all that were available for the 36 crews. I put in a little over 67hrs flying but only as a passenger as no navigational equipment was available. Maintenance must have been superb to keep these few planes flying night and day for we had no accidents. After about a month we moved to Sioux City, Iowa, and here, early in October, new B-24Ds were ferried in. Within a few days we were despatched to California and, at Hamilton Field, learned our destination was Hickham Field, Hawaii. Air Transport Command insisted that the trip be made in day formation with one of their planes leading the way. Our CO, Col William "Wild Bill" Matheny, however, was more insistent. He held out for the crossing to be made by single ships at night because the navigators needed the experience, which we certainly did. So the San Francisco-Honolulu flight was our first actual practice as B-24 navigators!'

'We left in our plane, *So Velly Sorry* on the night of 26 October and arrived at Hickham after a flight of 13½hrs. The crossing was perfect except for one incident. The front bomb-bay carried two extra fuel tanks with 400 gallons each. Our engineer tried to get the last drop and we momentarily lost all four engines when the switching somehow cut off their fuel. The movement of the Group's planes across 2,427 miles of ocean was spread over three or four nights during one of which the weather was bad in the vicinity of Hawaii. A B-24 disappeared on this particular night and many months passed before we knew its fate. It was finally found piled into a mountain on Oahu — the navigator's ETA was perhaps off and the let-down made too late.

'We were now under the 7th Air Force and from our base at Kahuku Field on Oahu most of our flight time was spent searching the Pacific up to 920 miles around the Hawaiin Islands for Japanese task forces. On one of these flights my squadron, the 372nd, lost its first crew and aircraft when they crashed into a local mountain in bad weather. Three thousand one hundred gallons of gasoline exploded on impact and

65
Capt Stanley 'Foxhole' Foster (left) and 1-Lt Clinton Roemer at Carney Field, Guadalcanal in the summer of 1943. Foster survived the rigours of war in the South Pacific only to die later as a result of a training accident in the States — a fate which also befell his crew's original co-pilot.

65

ten minutes later two of the six 500lb bombs went off. The Group suffered a number of other accidents around this time. I was witness to a ship from another squadron spin in from about a thousand feet off the edge of our field. It had an engine on fire, but it didn't appear the pilot was trying to make an emergency landing as the plane was headed away from Kahuku. One wing dropped and down the B-24 went, impacting top-side up in shallow water near the beach. Some Hawaiians managed to get inside and brought out the bodies while the plane was still burning. Over at another field a ship was demolished, though none of the crew was hurt, when it went into a gulch off the end of the runway.

'Something more ambitious than sea searches was being set up for us and on 22 December we were sent on our first bombing mission, a 1,500-mile dog leg west to the enemy anchorage at Wake Island, using Midway as a halfway refuelling stop. We approached in darkness at 8,000ft, peeled out of formation, gliding down to 2,500ft and released our bombs using a specially designed hand-held sight. The Colonel led in *So Velly Sorry*. The Japs must have been taken by surprise for their AA only began to fire just before our borrowed plane went over, fifth in line. During the long haul back to Midway we actually went from 24 December back to the 23rd, having crossed the international date line. Total flight time was 14½hrs. Following the raid one of our aircraft sent out on a photographic mission to Wake Island. The weather was bad and they flew around too long looking for Wake and ran out of fuel on the way back. Nothing was ever found. And there were other losses.

Before first light on 8 January, the 372nd's CO, Major Coxwell, took off with a crew from Barking Sands airport to participate in a mock attack on Pearl Harbor. The B-24 spun in 300yd off the end of the runway. All were killed. We had a very near miss ourselves one night. The co-pilot got smart and went through the pre-flight check list one night from memory. We got in the air and in a moment the pilot realised something was wrong, reached up and uncaged the gyro on the artificial horizon. We had been in a diving bank only a few feet off the water!

More sea searches for another month and then a dozen of our planes were sent south and eventually ended up with the 13th Air Force on Espiritu Santo in the New Hebrides, which is about a thousand miles east north east of Townsville, Australia. They had covered some 3,800 miles to get there.

'On 6 February it was our turn, one of six planes but the destination was Canton in the Phoenix Islands, a 1,911-mile trip. A Jap task force was supposedly in the vicinity of the Gilberts to the north west but we didn't locate anything when sent to search the ocean. Overloading was common on these long range patrols. The designers of the B-24 would have had heart attacks if they had known to what the plane was subjected. There were many occasions when we used every inch of the runway and barely struggled into the air. The first several hours of such flights were spent mushing through the air in a tail low position. It wasn't until enough gasoline has been burned up that the pilot could get the ship trimmed into a normal flying position. We arrived at the plane one morning to find the nose wheel off the ground and the plane resting on the little

66
Viewed through the navigator's window of another aircraft, B-24D 41-23929 'on the ramp' at Midway Island prior to the raid on Wake in December 1942.

67
The insignia on the Foster crew's B-24D, 41-23985, which was cannibalised after bomb blast damage. The origin of the nickname lay in the frequency of accidental Japanese air attacks on American property in China prior to World War 2 and the equally frequent broadcast apologies 'So very sorry'.

tail skid. We put as many men into the nose of the ship as it would hold, but to no avail. We taxied down the runway to take-off position dragging on the tail skid. While moving on to the runway the skid picked up the electrical wire connecting the field's landing lights and these we dragged with us all the way down the runway. With the nose cleared, the pilot and co-pilot stood on the brakes as hard as they could, poured full coal to the engines, released the brakes, the nose went down and away we went.

'After a week at Canton we moved to Santo to join the others, only to learn that we were supposed to have returned to Oahu as our squadron was being retained there. The 11th Bomb Group and its B-17s was to be withdrawn from the South Pacific — where it had been in action for six months — to re-form in Hawaii with B-24s, using the two remaining 307th Group Squadrons as a nucleus. Santo was really a rear base and for operations the Group flew the 642 miles to Henderson Field on Guadalcanal — which had just been retaken from the Japs.

'The 307th's first mission out of Guadalcanal was a fiasco and took place on 13 February, the day our crew arrived at Santo. Six B-24s and an equal number of fighters were sent to bomb a large Jap transport reported at anchor off Tonolei, Bougainville. The mission was planned by the new CO of the 11th Group who, fresh out from the States, was just as green as we were. (Colonel Matheny was still in Hawaii). A straight run at 15,000ft across Shortland Harbour, where most of the Jap fleet appeared to be, brought such a barrage of AA fire that two B-24s went down and another was so badly crippled that it lagged behind the formation, was shot up by Zeros and eventually had to ditch. Our formation was under attack by Zeros for well over two hours and four of the escort fighters were also lost. The Jap ship sank but it turned out to be a small freighter and not a transport. Thereafter most of our missions were flown at night in order to escape fighter interception. However, these didn't get off to a good start. Three nights after the disastrous first taste of combat, two B-24s returned from a mission to find Henderson Field closed in. They flew around waiting for the weather to improve and were eventually forced down when the gas ran out. One pilot baled his crew out and the other chose a water landing. Two men from each plane were killed. Bad weather could help or hinder friend and foe alike. The Japs would use heavy day cloud for sneak raids; on 21 February we lost *So Velly Sorry* when one of their aircraft dropped a bomb on the field at Santo. The blast blew the stump of a coconut tree through the B-24's rudder. With no replace-

68

68
Lt J. R. McCloskey's B-24D after having the tail turret grafted into the nose by the Hawaiian Air Depot. This aircraft, 41-23966, was an original of the 307th Bomb Group. Note the sea-search radar antenna below the pilot's window.

69
Nose turreted B-24D of 307th Bomb Group over Carney Field in the summer of 1943. Lower surfaces of the aircraft were painted black for night camouflage.

ment parts this became the Group's first plane to be cannibalised. This left the 307th Group with a total of 11 B-24Ds and 12 crews in its two squadrons — the 370th and 424th. For the next six months these two squadrons comprised the 13th Air Force's main heavy bomber force, although very soon undeserving of the description "force".

'The night missions were usually against shipping or airfields and in these attacks we would alternate with some Navy PB4Ys. Flares were often used to illuminate targets, these missions being co-ordinated with Navy TBF (torpedo bombers) who were to attack any ships seen. The Jap also made regular sorties over our base at night; we called him Washing Machine Charlie, a name derived from the noise created by his unsynchronised props. As a general rule he was quite harmless, merely keeping everyone awake, although on some occasions he did a great amount of damage. Henderson Field had no dispersal area and we always knew a few bombs correctly placed could do a lot of damage. It only took two bombs on the night of 23/24 March to just about put us out of the war. One bomb completely destroyed five B-24s and damaged all the rest of our planes (flat tyres, broken plexiglass, shrapnel holes, punctured gas tanks, etc). One of the planes destroyed was already under repair from an incident a few days earlier when a New Zealand Hudson ground looped and knocked off the B-24's tail. As we still had no spare parts all replacements had to come the 4,000 miles from Hawaii.

'At first light it was figured that by switching parts we might possibly have seven planes in commission by night but at 1000hrs only one plane was in, so the mission planned was called off — a 1,400-mile round trip to Nauru Island, bombing at dawn from 20,000ft. Two nights later the Nauru mission was run but not before another Hudson had ground looped with a depth charge on board exploding and damaging two of our already damaged planes. Only five B-24s were in shape to make the mission. At the end of the month we moved bag and baggage to Carney Field at Koli Point. The field wasn't quite complete but Col Matheney wanted to get us off Henderson before we lost any more planes because of the crowded conditions there. Washing Machine Charlie's lucky strike was, indirectly, to result in one more tragedy. One of the patched up B-24s was still being worked on at Carney when the crew chief learned it had been scheduled for a mission. He borrowed a jeep, drove to operations and pleaded with them to be allowed more time to check the plane out before it was put back on missions. His plea was in vain; there was no other B-24 available for the raid. On take-off the plane apparently lost power, spun in and the ensuing explosion of the gas load killed another complete crew.

'Replacement aircraft were not available until a month later and then only a very few. While I think we all approached the B-24 with a large amount of healthy respect, our losses were due predominantly to human error coupled with harsh operating conditions rather than to any inherent deficiencies in the plane.

'So that we could more safely operate in daylight, in April we were notified that our B-24s were to have radical armament modifications. The work could only be carried out at the Hawaiian Air Depot a few planes at a time. Our turn came in early May so back we flew across the Pacific island chain, 4,000 miles. The modifications consisted of fitting a B-17 type ball turret to the rear of the bomb-bay for underside defence. This had to retract to give ground clearance. The power tail turret was removed and installed in the nose while twin-hand controlled guns were put in the revised tail gun position. Some early primitive radar was also fitted for sea searching. It was early June before we got back to the 'Canal. An extra gunner now gave us a ten-man crew and our

70
Viewed from the waist window of another aircraft, B-24D 41-24012 wings its way up the 'slot' (the passage between the Solomon Islands) in the summer of 1943.

first day mission with the new armament was quite eventful.

On 12 June our crew and another were despatched at 0800hrs on a shipping prowl between Buka and Rabaul. We carried six 1,000lb bombs with delay action fuses. If anything was spotted we were to make a minimum altitude skip bombing attack. The other crew was brand new — this was their first mission. Our route was up the west side of the Solomons — flying 20 miles off shore — to Buka, thence over to a point near Rabaul and return by the same way. About 300 miles out, halfway along the coast of Bougainville, the gunners reported two planes approaching us high and fast from the rear. At first we thought they were Zeros but as they drew nearer we could distinguish two engines and then thought they were the new twin-engine fighters. As they came closer still we recognised them as Mitsubishi "Betty" bombers. It was obvious that they were intent on interception. Foster waited until they were nearly up with us, then did a steep 90 degree turn which split the Bettys, one on either side. Then the shooting started. Our top turret gunner drew first blood by shooting out the starboard engine of the Betty on our left. The Jap began a descending 180° turn to the left and headed back home. In the meantime the other crew had managed to knock a few pieces off the other Betty and he too did a 180° heading for home.

'By now Foster was pretty mad and very definitely out for blood so we turned and went out for the cripple. We caught him just barely skimming the water and with a few more bursts from nose and top turrets forced him in. Then we started chasing the other Betty who had been circling a little way off watching the show. He turned and started making a beeline for the airfield at Buka. After about a five minute chase it became evident that if we were to catch him it would be over Buka. Not having any desire to take on the entire Jap contingent there, we made another 180° turn back to find the downed Betty. We were very much surprised to find it still floating and four men standing on the wing trying to inflate a rubber raft. As the Japs regularly shot-up our downed or parachuting fliers, in retaliation we gave them the same treatment. On our first strafing run we sank the Betty and probably got three of the Jap for when we came back for our next run we could locate only one Jap in the water who appeared to be breaking every known swimming record in an attempt to get away. With our bombs still aboard, we flew towards Rabaul and then returned to the scene of battle hoping to find that a seaplane had been sent out to pick up any survivors, but no such luck. After our return to the 'Canal, we learned that the Japs had sent a fighter sweep to the Russell Islands that day, so when we went by Bougainville the Bettys were probably all they could send after us. If it hadn't been for that we no doubt would have been intercepted by a swarm of Zeros and that would have been a different story indeed. Upon examining our plane we found no damage whatsoever. The other crew had a few holes in theirs of which most were .50in. The gunners, in their excitement, had put a few through their own rudders. When an ammunition count was made it was found the new crew had fired almost twice as much as we had.

'Around this time the Group received its first replacement crews and a few others in July, but four of these were lost almost immediately. I think that these losses can largely be attributed to navigation and pilot error. The new crews coming out from the United States thought they knew it all and arrived with the attitude that they were going to show us how to win the war. One pilot announced that if jumped by Zeros he would immediately turn out to sea and the fighters would soon turn around and go home. That was sound, sure; but he went further by saying he would do the same thing even if in formation as his chances would still be better — which was plain unadulterated nonsense. If that was what they were teaching them in the States they'd have been better sending them down without any training — they would have lived longer.

'Well, this pilot did what he said he would do and another new crew went right along with him. A formation of nine planes had been jumped by a lone Zero. The two B-24s with new crews broke formation and the Zero went along with them — better to play tag with two than seven. No telling what happened for neither B-24 ever came back. It looked like pure pilot error but perhaps the little Zero gave them a merry chase and got them lost.

'Another replacement crew was missing on

71

71
Tragedy. The burning remains of Lt 'Raunchy' Miller's B-24 which 'spun in' shortly after take-off on 29 April 1943. Eight men perished. The cause, possible loss of power on one engine at lift off. Miller was reckoned one of the best pilots in the 307th. Six B-24s were despatched on this particular mission to bomb a native village at the request of a Coastwatcher (the term for individuals who reported enemy air and sea movements to the Allies) on Bougainville. Four of the bombers had to turn back when bad weather was encountered and only 'Foxhole' Foster's aircraft managed to get through and make the attack. It helped the Coastwatcher for only a few days and then the natives were back on the side of the Japs and he was on the run.

a night mission. The weather was clear but the navigator became lost and the plane flew round in circles until out of gas when it had to ditch. The navigator was the only one who paid with his life in the ditching. Yet another new crew that didn't come back from a night mission was later found to have flown into a 1,000ft mountain. The weather was perfect and again it looked like pilot or navigator error. The night missions could be suicide if you didn't know what the score was. We were laughed at many times by the new crews in trying to help them. They would listen politely with that know-it-all look on their faces and then go blissfully on their own way.

'One of the worst traps were cloud shadows on the water. From high altitudes they often looked more like islands and atolls than the real things — and this was true both night and day. Many crews were probably lost chasing cloud shadows when they should have been trusting navigation.

'Before our B-24Ds were modified I navigated from the nose; after modification from a table on the flight deck directly behind the pilot and facing forwards. On search missions, shipping prowls or long daylight flights I was kept pretty busy. Navigation was strictly dead reckoning which demanded constant drift readings, double drifts to check wind direction and velocity, along with occasional sun-lines when possible. Searches were flown at a maximum altitude of 1,000ft and flight duration could be from eight to 13hrs — all out of sight of land. Night navigation was not so confining as by day. On long flights it was only necessary to take a three-star fix about once an hour unless there was an indication of flying through an area of shifting winds. As I could shoot and plot a three-star fix in less than 15min, there was nothing to do until time to take the next one.

'Navigation in the Solomons was much easier both day and night. Before the nose turret was put in, forward visibility for the navigator was wide and good. With the move to the flight deck the outlook was severely restricted. The long hauls were fatiguing due to the continuous high noise level and constant vibration — my navigation equipment would move across the table if not secured. As we flew to our targets at a respectable altitude and only climbed before bombing we were never high long enough to begin getting cold. The men in the rear of the ship did wear the heavy fleece-lined clothing but up front we wore only our sun tans, sometimes with flight coveralls over them or our leather flight jackets. During my service steel helmets were never worn and body armour was not available. In my missions our plane was hit a number of times but far less than many of the others in our group. We were lucky in never having any injuries. A piece of flak bounced off our pilot's boot, another lump went through a bag of flight clothes our bombardier was sitting on — right between his legs! The top turret gunner had a scratch across his forehead from a piece of spent flak that broke through the plexiglass and another piece left a black smudge across our tail gunner's cheek.

'On daylight flights we were usually met by Zeros which outnumbered us anything from three to six to one. We had fighter escort over the Solomons but this was generally "sucked off" by one formation of Zeros while another waited to jump us. With the modified armament the B-24D was not deficient in firepower.

'I flew my last mission, as lead navigator, on 14 September, when we gave the big Jap airfield at Kahili its biggest pasting. At this date, of the nine crews of 372nd Bomb Squadron that had left the US a year before, half had been killed, the rest broken up or transferred. Foster's crew were veterans in an outfit now filled out with replacements. Early in October I learned that I was going home. After all I had been through in B-24s I was none too happy to have to make the trip back to the States navigating a retired B-17!'

Round Trip To Hell

Walter Cronkite/William Dabney

In the annals of Liberator operations Ploesti stands without par. For United States war strategists destruction of Hitler's major oil source was a war-winning panacea worth the air strike gamble of high losses. The first day of August 1943 witnessed the despatch from North Africa by the 9th Air Force of a maximum effort Liberator force made up of its own two groups and three from the 8th Air Force. Of the 179 B-24Ds that set out 53 did not come back. The target was left in flames but the hurt to Germany's fuel supplies was not as lasting as was hoped. Bravery was the hall-mark of this dramatic and spectacular raid and in the aftermath several newsmen sought to record the experiences of survivors. Walter Cronkite, the premier anchorman of postwar US television, was then a staff writer for United Press, covering the war against Germany. From his conversations with a co-pilot in the 44th Bomb Group he compiled this graphic account, presented here just as it was penned in 1943:

Bill Dabney hails from Louisville, Kentucky. He looks a little like the kid next door who, fresh out of college, tries to make you his first customer for a 5,000 dollar annuity. He's clean-shaven, eager, sold on his product — which right now happens to be bombing the Axis to its knees. And for that product he's finding plenty of customers. His sales-room is the co-pilot's seat of the fat-bellied, four-motored Liberator *Buzzin' Bear*.

Way back early last summer those of us who were covering the Eighth Air Force in the British Isles were a little surprised to notice the few squadrons of Liberators then over here skimming along at roof-top height over the English countryside.

Obviously they were on practice missions but even the crews themselves didn't know what they were practising — except low-level flying. These high-atltitude machines that had been bombing Germany from 25,000ft looked a little out of their element at 'zero' feet. There was a lot of speculation among the correspondents, and among the crews themselves, as to the meaning of the new training.

'Maybe they're going to try to sneak us to Berlin on the deck,' Dabney suggested one night when I was visiting him on his base.

That wasn't the answer, but it was two months later before all the world was let in on the secret. Meanwhile I'd returned to Dabney's base only to find that all the machines were gone, all the pilots and co-pilots and bombardiers and navigators and gunners cleared out. Where they had gone was just another mystery in the long series.

Where they had gone was Africa — somewhere in that desert stretch that Montgomery had cleared of the Nazis only a few months before.

Down there they studied scale-model replicas built on sand-tables of strange country. They studied topographical features. They studied miniatures built in wood of oil fields and refineries until their eyes ached.

They then went out and practised bombing mock-up villages and industries built in the African desert by intelligence officers who had reproduced every identifying feature and every target.

The target, of course, was Ploesti, source of one-third of Hitler's oil, source of practically all the high-octane gasoline his beleaguered armies were using on the Russian front.

When the boys returned from that raid they had only praise for the intelligence officers' perfection in duplicating the countryside and built-up areas of Romania. But they pointed out that one thing, one important thing, was lacking from the sand-table models from the mock-ups on the African desert.

That was the flame of Ploesti. There were acres of fire after the first pair of Liberators had crossed the target. Great, billowing clouds of it. Smoke was so thick it looked as if it could tear the wings off the Liberators.

The lads on those planes flew into hell. Some of them were lucky and flew out again. A lot didn't. The fires they themselves had started licked up and crumpled them like a candle-flame withering a moth.

But this is Bill Dabney's story. There is no fanfare to his yarn. There are no writer's tricks, no furbelows. It is set down just as Bill tells it — just as most of these guys who laugh when you call them heroes tell their stories.

You are sitting around the so-called 'club' in Nissen hut mess on an airfield somewhere in England. Every once in a while somebody in a leather flight jacket leans forward and pokes the dying embers in the pot-bellied stove.

And slowly the story comes out:

'We all figured it was going to be one of two extremes. It was either going to be nice and easy — or rougher than hell. And from the send-off we got, we decided it was going to be the latter.

'We had just taken off and were beginning our circle of the field waiting for the others to come up and join us when a pillar of flames and smoke sprang up from one of our satellite fields. It was the white smoke of bombs and the black smoke of gasoline.

'Captain William R. Cameron, our pilot from Hanford, California, looked at me and I looked at him and we didn't have to say anything. We knew some unlucky guy from one of the other squadrons didn't make the take-off. We knew because we'd sweated out some anxious seconds ourselves getting that heavy fuel load off the ground.

'Bill broke the silence to take the words right out of my mouth. "My God, what a way to start a mission".

'It was a Sunday morning, but not like those quiet Sunday mornings back in Louisville or Hanford. We knew we were taking off on one of the most important raids of the war. We knew it had been tried three times before with very little success and that this time everything depended on us.

'We had been briefed for weeks on every aspect of the job. Movies, lectures, and highly detailed scale models of Ploesti and the surrounding country had made us familiar with the town as if we had lived there ourselves. In the desert a full-sized skeleton model of the refineries was erected, and day after day, at zero feet, we dropped dummy bombs on the outlines of the cracking plant and storage tanks.

'A few days before the raid, Major General Lewis E. Brereton had come from Cairo to emphasis again the importance of the mission.

' "This job," he told us, "by use of ground troops would take an entire army many months of bloody fighting. You men are going to do it from the air in a single day. This is a dangerous mission, but we feel that if the refineries are demolished, and the entire force wiped out, it will still be worth the price."

'We knew just about what that price would be.

'As soon as we'd pulled our squadron into a snug position in the formation, I called Sergeant Gerald Sparks of Meridian, Mississippi, our radio operator on the intercom. That really is his name "Sparks".

' "How about a little hot jive on the way over, Sparky?" I asked.

' "Seven-thirty is a little early sir, but I'll try," he laughed.

'Sparky himself was a real musician, and every night we'd sit under the Libyan moon while he played on his guitar and sang. In the early stages of our missions, he'd always get some Itie or Jerry station blasting hot American swing between propaganda stories, and Bill and I would lean back and grin like hell and say, "If the boys back home could only see us now!"

'About eleven-fifty we saw the first rocky crags that make up the chain of islands off the Greek coast. We were flying a fairly loose formation now, as far as we could see, were echelons of B-24s, stretched across the topaz waters of the Mediterranean.

'Then suddenly those waters gave birth to a cone of smoke that rose from a widening circle of waves. The smoke was that tell-tale white and black again.

' "Christ, another one," called Captain Jim DeVinney, from Atlantic City, our bombardier.

'Almost at the same time a ship from the formation on our left swings out in front of us with two port engines out. We saw his bomb-bay doors open and his bombs drop into the sea as he lightened the load of his two good engines for the long headlong dash home. The engine-eating sand of the desert had claimed another victim and I guess we all gave a little prayer for the boys in that ship.

'It was almost too much to take. The gods just didn't seem to be with us. So many bad breaks, so early in the game was pretty disheartening.

'We were starting our climb now, a long tedious climb to 15,000 feet in order to clear the peaks of Greece and Yugoslavia. I called the boys in the back to tell them that we were going up so that they could get a little oxygen in the event any of them needed it. The weather ahead didn't look very inviting. We were pushing into leaden, anvil-headed cumulus clouds that spelled rough weather, and our wing men drew up a little closer in hopes we wouldn't lose them in the muck.

'Bill and I watched our engine instruments with hopeful eyes. The climbs had always meant trouble for our engines, and we were really sweating this one out. Every foot of the way. An abortive, or turn back, would mean an ignominious end to all our plans, we nursed the *Buzzin' Bear* along with careful hands.

'Slowly we got our altitude, and I called Frank Maruszewski, our tail gunner, from Uniontown, Pennsylvania, to check on the boys in our formation.

' "Right on the old agate, Sir," he called, "The number three man is a little wide, but he'll be okay."

'The mountains weren't getting any smaller by this time. They reminded me of the towering Rockies of Colorado. Away off to our left, dodging in and out of the clouds, we could see the other group, but they were drawing further and further away as we flew on.

'The intercom buzzed. "Fighter at ten o' clock, two thousand above," called Sergeant Gola Gibby, our top turret man from Madisonville, Tennessee.

'Bill looked at me and the question was written in his eyes. Had we been spotted already? Were they sending up fighters this far from the target?

'Anything could happen now and we could hear the gunners rattling out a test round getting their guns ready.

' "It's just an old crate, Sir," laughed Gibby again, and sure enough plowing through the clouds above was an ancient biplane.

' "I'll bet that baby's more scared than we are," Jim called, and we all felt better and settled down again.

'At last the signal for the let-down came, and Tom Clifforn from Upper Darby, Pennsylvania, our navigator, called to say we were a little off course and he hoped like hell we'd come out at the right place.

'Down we went, so I pulled back the rpm's to help keep us in position, but even so we slid on by the *Suzy Q* the group leader flown by Major William H. Brandon of Nashville, and Colonel Leon W. Johnson of Moline, Kansas, our group commander.

'For an awful moment we had terrible visions of ruining the whole deal by messing up the formation, but finally *Suzy* pulled ahead and Cameron called for more power so we swung back into position.

'The weather was clearing now, and stretched out ahead lay the green fields of Romania — a lush countryside that looked like Paradise after the dust bowl we had left that morning.

' "Pilot to Navigator," Tom was on the intercom again.

' "Speak, Slave," barked Bill. We always got a hell of a kick out of that, and it seemed funnier than ever today when we were all so keyed up.

' "The Danube should be below pretty soon now, and after that we'll cross the low country for about an hour and half."

'We all rubber-necked like a bunch of tourists hoping to add the famous blue river to the list of scenic wonders we'd seen. But the muddy waters we saw might just as well have been the Ohio, Mississippi, or any big river back home. In fact, we'd a devil of a lot rather seen the Ohio, Mississippi or any big river back home right then.

'The group levelled out at 3,000ft for the trip to the hills above the target, and we searched the sky for enemy fighters.

'Every few minutes we'd pass over a country town with its dusty streets and avenues of trees. It was hard to believe we were deep inside Europe in a strange country. This might have been Indiana and little Indiana country towns. The little groups of people watching us as we roared over, would be gaping just like that back home.

'I guess we worried the navigator a lot in those last minutes. Every little while somebody would call and ask how far it was to the IP (Initial Point where we would turn in to make the bombing run), but Tom was steady as a rock and patiently answered us in his usual exact manner. Before coming to us he had been with the RAF and was a veteran of the block-busting shows on Essen, Cologne and Berlin.

'At 2.15 Tom said we would hit the target in another half-hour, so I called the crew and told everybody to check their guns and bombs. The waist gunners, Ernest McCabe, another Meridian boy, and Gerald Street from Urbanette, Arkansas, each had a box of incendiaries to toss out and we wanted to be plenty certain they delivered them where they'd do the most harm.

'Cameron then asked me to take over for a while, so he could adjust his flak suit, helmet and chute. Our pilots didn't ordinarily wear the armoured vests for high altitude work but today we were going to be on the deck and we figured any extra protection might help.

'The IP was just as we'd memorised it — a ridge of green mountains sprinkled with oil derricks which dotted a trail down to the plain and to Ploesti itself. The only thing we hadn't seen before were the guns, which appeared in every field and patch of woods; even the houses fell apart, revealing heavy flak guns, and way up ahead we could see men hastily setting up positions between the derricks.

' "Get ready, boys, this is it!" Bill called, and those were the last words we heard before the run.

'We turned 90% degrees to the right, dropped in directly behind Brandon to begin the dive to the target.

'Then we saw the hell ahead!

'Ploesti was an inferno of black, flame-filled muck, surrounded by a white layer of smoke screen. Not a section of our target was visible through the flames, and we could see great balls of fire leaping up as the oil storage tanks exploded.

'But Colonel Johnson and Major Brandon went on until we hit ground level about three miles from town. Suddenly black puffs of heavy flak blossomed ahead, but they were high and scattered. Then I looked down.

'From the fields below, streams of tracers lined the sky ahead, and from patches of woods on our right came continuous blasts of light flak shells. It was too amazing, too fearful.

'I could see few gun positions and very little camouflage, but they were certainly shooting and those peaceful pastures seemed alive with yellow tracer trails.

'On our right a train of tank cars loomed up, so close I had only to look out of my window to see it. Behind these cars the enemy had set up gun positions and the tracks seemed ablaze with fire from their muzzles.

'Our top turret snarled, and I smelled the cordite from the nose guns as the boys raked the cars up and down. A second later and their shots had taken effect. The whole damned train seemed to disintegrate in one fierce explosion.

'Undismayed by the flames that seemed to lick our very wingtips, Brandon still was bearing down on the target, and we had short glimpses of smoke stacks and the cracking plant silhouetted against the sheet of raging fire.

'There were planes all around us. The ships of Colonel John "Killer" Kane's outfit were going in on our left, and on the right our other squadrons were dimly outlined in the smoke.

'Then it came. Between two pillars of blazing oil we crossed the refinery amid the greatest destruction imaginable.

'Looking up at the diving, twisting ships, I saw in one awful second a ball of fire where a bomber had been a moment before. Just ahead another shuddered and pulled almost straight up as the pilot made his last effort to save his crew from the stricken ship. They went up almost a thousand feet before the doomed plane lost its momentum and fell like a fiery coffin.

'Our own *Buzzin' Bear* was hot as an oven and I glanced at the air temperature gauge — it had passed the last mark! But the flak suit felt pretty wonderful and the chute reassuring.

72

72
At 200ft the last flight of 44th Bomb Group B-24s approaches the Columbia Aquila Romana refinery at Ploesti as leading flights disappear through smoke and flames. Another group, unable to locate its own target, had earlier attacked this plant and the defences were alerted when the 44th arrived.
via J. Archer

'I started to call Jim to see if the bombs had gone, but just then Brandon pulled up abruptly and we saw three tall smoke stacks pass under our wing as the target appeared for a brief second.

'Now we were in a diving turn to the right, and there was blue sky ahead as the wind cleared the smoke. It didn't clear for long. The green fields below were suddenly alive again with belching guns, and I could see the sweat-stained German gunners furiously following us with their barrels.

'This was the end. We were too low to turn, and it would be suicide to pull up. Lordy, Lordy, I would have sold out for two cents as I watched the flames leap from the forest of black barrels.

'We had no defence, I thought, but I didn't reckon with fast-thinking Johnson and Brandon. They dived so low that the gunners abandoned their triggers and ducked as we roared over where their heads had been a second before.

'Now there was blue sky ahead, the wind was against us and we had left the fires and were skimming the tops of the waving corn.

'Bill called for less throttle, so I pulled her back, glancing quickly at the engine instruments to see if we'd been hit — but they were perking like the old cabriolet back home and by some miracle we were still going strong.

'I was just mentally patting myself on the back when it all began again. Out of nowhere 20 fighters appeared, coming straight at us in a long dive. I prayed that we were too low for anything but a passing shot as they went over. But three of the bastards were heading right for us.

'The top turret roared and in a flash they had passed — not over, but under! And we thought *we* were on the deck!

'The ship vibrated as the waist guns chattered, and from the tail Frank cursed the Jerrie's passing speed.

'Bill pulled up behind the Colonel again, and we looked hopefully for our wing men in anticipation of the fighters' return.

'And back they came. More this time from all directions. I could see Messerschmitt 109s, 110s and 210s, and once a lumbering Dornier 217 seemed to be racing us.

'I called for the top turret, but Gibby only answered, "Three on our tail", and we knew he had problems of his own.

'A Liberator off to our right was beating off repeated attacks when all at once it

73

View from a departing 44th Bomb Group Liberator as the last flights come across the target. Some smoke screen pots have been ignited along an avenue of trees (white smoke). An unaccompanied horse can be seen in the road (bottom right corner) its rider apparently having taken cover behind a bank.
via J. Archer

seemed to skim the ground; then in a cloud of dust it skidded miraculously to a stop.

'On beyond an Me 110 fell in a flaming heap and an Me 109 did a fiery cartwheel through the wheat.

'Now the fight was slowing down to a walk. Out in front I saw a white pillbox and called Jim and Tom to strafe it, but as we came closer we saw a Red Cross on its dome and we roared by in peace.

'Bill looked wonderfully relieved, and I shook myself and checked the instruments again. We were just skimming the fields and isolated trees when Bill said, with his first smile, "Let's go between those two ahead".

'We clipped a few leaves and Bill hollered with joy. "This is the most fun I've had since flying school," he said.

'Personally I couldn't go that strong, but we were alive and still had an airplane and there were no tracers and fire any longer.

'We expected the fighters to attack again though, so for the next 70 miles we stayed at tree-top level, only pulling up when we crossed the Danube and were approaching the mountains again. I looked out to check the formation and found we had only two planes left in the squadron.

'On our right Charley Henderson of Dallas limped along with a gaping hole in his left rudder. On the other side, Jim Hill of Midlands, Texas, was holding his own pretty well.

'Up ahead Brandon was beginning to climb, as we eased up behind him and started the long haul back over the hills and across to the sea. The minutes crawled by, and we prayed that the *Bear* would survive the climb and that our gas would hold out for a few hours more.

'The mountains ended and blue water stretched out ahead. We were really sweating out our gas by now. Bill called Tom to check our estimated time of arrival at base, and then he answered in his usual matter-of-fact RAF manner: "If the petrol holds out, Skipper, our ETA is 2130."

'This shook us pretty badly, since it would mean a total elapsed flying time of 14 hours — right at the limit of our gas capacity — but we prayed some more and throttled back to conserve fuel.

'Brandon was our only company now. Henderson and Hill had dropped back to save their sputtering engines. Suddenly a battered wreck we recognised as the ship of Reg Carpenter crossed between us and fired a red Very cartridge.

' "He's in trouble", called Jim.

'That was a useless remark. We could see the hundreds of holes that dotted the rear of Carpenter's ship.

' "P-Peter from R-Robert," Reg called on the radio. "Can you slow down a little? I'm having trouble."

'We were almost stalling out as it was, but Bill eased her back until we mushed along at 145 hoping Red could hold out a few minutes longer.

'Then I saw the most welcome sight of my life - the grey shores of Africa under the darkening sky. We were home! The crew screamed and raved. We'd made it in one piece and ahead was safety and peace and quiet.

'When we landed "Pappy" (Major Howard W. Moore of Farmersburg, Indiana, and our squadron commander who had already completed his tour of duty) gave Bill and me one hell of a bear hug.

' "I didn't think you'd made it," he cried, and we all slapped each other again and roared happily off to interrogation in his Jeep.

'There were some amazing stories that night and for many days to come!

'How Jim Hill cut a balloon cable and never felt the jar as it hit his wing and snapped. George Martin, who drove straight through a five-strand high-tension line but lived to tell the tale. Then there was one of "Killer" Kane's boys who flew so low he bumped the ship on the ground and dented the nose. There were many more just as thrilling, just as frightening.

'Reg Carpenter and his crew never made the shore that night, but ditched in the sea with a load of wounded men. The boys spent 29 cruel hours in a dinghy before they finally were rescued by an RAF launch in an amazing night operation.

'Well, that's how rough a trip it was. A lot of men died doing their part. Bombing is our business, and this was a big deal with a lot of complications. All of us were eager to go, and some of the men who were lost had been relieved from combat, but went because they hated to miss a good show.

'Whatever praise, whatever glory is due goes to our pals who died. They took the brunt of the attack. They absorbed the hell we survived.'

74
Shattered Sunday. Ploesti refinery installations burn as Liberators leave for the long and dangerous trip back to Africa.
via J. Archer

74

On The Bad End

Garner Williams

'Experience shaped my feelings for the Liberator. Guess if I had gotten the same experiences with any other airplane I would feel the same way about that. Who knows.

'I got into Navy aviation in 1943 and trained as a mechanic and air gunner. One evening during the final phase a bunch of us were waiting outside a camp shack where we could shoot pool. The door hadn't been unlocked so we just stood there talking. An Army B-24 flew over with gear down and we guessed it was running up to a turn in for our field. One of the guys noticed the ship had an outer engine stopped and the prop feathered and we all took more interest and otherwise probably wouldn't have been watching as the plane started to make a turn in towards the runway. So happened it was also turning in on the dead engine and that wing dropped and kept dropping. The pilot must have pushed the power on the good engines as there was a sudden roar, only instead of the wing picking up it tucked right under, the plane was on its back and just power dived into the ground. Blew like a bomb: Must have been a mile from where we were but I swear we felt the concussion. No one got out. They said it was 100% pilot error; all I know is that it made clear to me how in a matter of seconds a good flying airplane could become a death trap.

'Don't recall that the incident gave me any qualms when I was crewed up on a PB4Y-1. That was the designation the Navy gave the B-24; she still went by the name Liberator although it wasn't much used. We were sent out to Hawaii as a replacement for a patrol bomber squadron. It was a trip I won't forget. At the end of the first hop we had pulled on to the ramp and were getting personal gear out of the rear of the ship when an Army B-24 made a take-off. Funny, even when you have little knowledge of engines you know when one doesn't sound right and I guess we all turned to watch this ship. It lifted clear of the runway and the gear started to tuck up when there was a mild detonation. Immediately the left wing dropped but just when it looked as if it would strike the ground it began to come back up. What happened then our crew could not agree on. I think the B-24 had lost height when an engine blew and just flew into the ground; others said that the left wing hit a small boulder. Whatever it was the result was a sliding, busting heap of metal that came to a stop in a great ball of flame. Only the two gunners in the rear of the ship got out and one was so badly burned he died next day. Two firefighters who tried to get near the inferno were also hospitalised.

'I didn't sleep easy that night and I'd be lying if I didn't admit to being more than a little worried when our ship took off next morning. In a few weeks I'd witnessed two terrible examples of what could happen to an airplane when things went wrong — and it was the type of airplane I was riding! We had a long flight ahead, all over water, and we pulled up to about 8,000ft and stayed there. The ocean looked calm and despite the ever present vibration and noise the flight was pleasant, particularly as the waist guns were stowed and the window shutters fitted. Stretched out on sailor bags I was trying to read some supposedly red-hot banned novel that had been passed around the crew and looked as if every other crew in the Navy had passed it around too.

'A few hours out the sunlight suddenly stopped flooding in the waist windows and a glance told me we were in cloud. We went in and out of cloud and then seemed to be really stuck with it. We were still sliding through overcast when I decided to visit the jon. Just got to my feet when — wham! Suddenly I was spread against the side of the fuselage, my world started tumbling. Despite the dizziness the immediate automatic reaction was to reach for a parachute but I couldn't move an arm! Not that the 'chute was where it had been placed; I quickly saw the 'chute, bags and other loose items were with me, pinned to the fuselage side by the extreme G forces. People will tell you that at times like this you don't have time to be frightened . . . To hell with that tale; I was terrified. All I could think of was that the ship was falling out of the sky and that at any moment the sea would take over. While pinned down by that great invisible hand I recall one of those soft Navy hats got floating leisurely by and thinking how could that happen. Then gradually Williams, 'chute and all the other stuff began to slide down to heap up on the deck. I could move again and in panic tried to kick free of bag straps in which my legs were entangled. At last the precious 'chute was clipped on and about the same time sanity returned. Looking round I saw the ball gunner laughing at me, which had an immediate shaming effect.

'Standing up and squinting out of the window I could see the ocean where I wanted to see it, a few hundred feet below and at the right angle! The rest of the trip was, as they say, without incident. My first experience of G forces had apparently happened because in changing over control the pilots had somehow stalled the ship and lost 5,000ft before, thankfully, they managed to pull her out. The airplane suffered several popped rivets and we never flew it again. There was some story that the wings were bent but don't know if there was any truth in it.

'Eventually we joined our squadron and started flying long lone 12hr patrols over the ocean. We were assigned areas where the likelihood of encountering enemy shipping or aircraft was remote and the flights were always made at fairly low altitude. We usually carried a mixed bag of ordnance in the bomb-bay in case Jap ships or subs were sighted but on the first four missions I saw nothing but waves and more waves. On our fifth trip we were coming home when I heard the skipper say he was going to climb; there was a weather front ahead and he was going to go around it. From the waist windows I couldn't see much of what lay ahead until we were in a climbing turn and got a look at what I would call a mighty big thunderhead brewing up in our path.

'Soon all I could see on one side of the ship was these too pretty clouds as we tried to fly around the storm. How high we had gotten when they engulfed us the pilots never did divulge but things quickly got rough. Rain then hail was spraying in the waist. Again, how long we were in the overcast I couldn't say when all at once I knew something was wrong. That first shot of fear had me straight on to my 'chute. The ball gunner did likewise and he wasn't laughing this time. (The pilots had retracted the ball turret before we went into the storm). Then there was that helplessness that follows the initial G pull and once again we were gripped by centrifugal force and nailed to the floor. Only this time, one moment you could move, the next you couldn't; not that either of us would have baled out into that wild wide ocean. And again after an eternity of fear we were out of it, skimming over the sea through torrential rain. The tail gunner came stumbling out of his turret; white faced he shouted in my ear an obscenity-laced threat that he would not fly with our skipper again. When we landed there was some hard words between the navigator and the PPC (Patrol Plane Commander — pilot). We air gunners had to hold our mouths. Hard to believe, but they said severe icing was the cause of that second plunge.

'There had always been a personality clash between the men up front and after this incident the squadron commander must have decided to make changes; anyway, the crew was split up. I filled in on an experienced crew whose tail gunner had gone sick. We did several missions, the same old monotonous sea-prowls, a safe kind of war to be in but I found I was becoming more and more apprehensive just about flying.

'Well, I finally did get to see the hot end of the war, in quite a spectacular and traumatic way.

'We were about half way through a patrol when there was a lot of excited talk up front. I didn't pick it all up over the inter-phone but seems we had come across a small Jap convoy. Our skipper said we were going in to attack and that all gunners were to rake the ships with our 50-calibres as we passed. He took the Liberator way down until we must have been just above the wave tops. Up front they really poured on the power as the sensation of speed was terrific. I was flying waist gunner and peering over the top of my gun I saw a ship flash by, looked like a small coastal vessel, only too far off to be in range.

Then there was a distorted shout over the inter-phone and the next instant smoke and fumes swept past my face. I turned and was horrified to see a mass of flames coming around the bomb-bay bulkhead and another member of the crew stumbling towards me. I don't think I had time for any mental reaction because everything happened so quickly. The rear of the airplane suddenly dropped; there was a violent shock and water swept me backwards but I managed to cling on the gun handle and stop myself being pushed towards the tail. There followed another tremendous rendering of metal, the rear of the plane dropped away further but as it did I saw blue sky appear in the left waist where I clung. When death looks you in the face the efforts to escape him are your all. I went through that window like a bolt of lightning, oblivious that I'd snagged an arm, probably on the gun sight, or that the primary or secondary impact had somehow smashed my left leg.

'At least I was a powerful swimmer and soon broke surface to see a crew raft floating a short distance away. Reaching the side I was surprised to feel a hand grasp me under the arm; it was the radio man. With his help I managed to struggle aboard. The plane had completely disappeared and all there was was another raft and the ball gunner who soon joined us. We were the only three survivors and, like me, the others could only guess at what downed us. Fact is we never did know what happened although it seems a good bet the Liberator took some Jap flak. Strangely there was no sign of any ships and yet we must have crashed in full view of them. I was in pretty bad shape with some nasty cuts and a leg that was giving me hell. The ball gunner had a few minor burns and the radio man didn't have a scratch. They pumped morphine into me and things began to whirl. Sometime before sunset the other guys were all excited and while I don't recall seeing it another Liberator spotted our float and circled. About noon next day the Navy fished us out. Again I don't remember much but my leg was set and a day later I was transferred to a hospital ship which was going back to the States. Just why and where it happened I don't know and never asked! We came into San Francisco and after a few weeks in a Navy hospital I finally wound-up in a shore-based job. The other two survivors went back to flying and after the war I learned both were listed as missing.

'I've flown a lot since, fact I couldn't do my job if I didn't fly. No fears — I think no more of boarding a jet than I do getting into a car. A friend who did a tour on B-24s in China and professes to love the old ship says what happened to me was all on the bad end of flying the plane. He can say that again! A few years back I happened to be on an airport where there was an airshow going on. What should I see looking out the terminal building but a Liberator sitting on the ramp. One glance was enough to make a chill run up my spine.'

75
Nautical Lib. In adopting and adapting the upstart Army Air Forces' B-24 for oceanic patrol and strike, the US Navy stamped its mark well and truly on the type. Under their nomenclature it became a PB4Y-1 (Patrol Bomber type 4 from Consolidated — Y being code for this manufacturer — model 1). A different make of nose turret was preferred and there were many internal equipment changes in the cause of navalisation. The Liberator pilot became a PPC — Patrol Plane Commander. *General Dynamics*

Sea Prowl

Al Hamel

In the Pacific war zones US Navy Liberators and Privateers flew regular long range armed patrols seeking Japanese shipping. This record of one such mission, told in the airman's language of those days, was made by Al Hamel, Plane Captain and Engineer:

'Take-off for the patrol was set for 0200. This meant getting up at 0030, a fast chow down, preflighting — getting rations aboard; firing up the old Homelite power plant; starting up No 3 and getting whiffs of 115/145 avgas as you overprimed, then lots of white smoke as it leaned out and caught, hoping that you didn't have to use the fire bottle.

'With all four turning, it was like being in a boxcar on the worst rail line. Then each engine checked out — mags at 2,000 turns, 50 to 75 RPMs was pretty good drop off — over a hundred you leaned out to clear the plugs. Then each up to 2,700 and 52in HG — using the turbos to set take-off power.

'With all the ammo, bombs and depth charges — full load of 3,000gal of fuel, down the runway we started. It was Marston steel matting. Christ what a roar! Airborne up with the gear selector — the emergency hydraulic pump whining away to help out the old Vickers pump on No 3. Ka-lump — the gear selector slams to the neutral and the after station reports gear up. Plane Captain bounces down to the nose wheel to check on how things are there — but you don't touch the wheel, it would really tear you up spinning like that. Meanwhile, the flaps are milked up. RPMs reduced to 2,400 and 48in HG to climb out.

'At altitude, back on the 1830's to 2,200 and 32in — leaning each engine using those old big flowmeter needles that jumped around like an ant. Next, check out the turrets an waist guns. With each of them pounding away the smell of burnt powder fills the air. With stoppages cleared lookouts report manned and ready — the long watch begins.

'Props are synched from time to time and you can hear the slightest RPM difference. Navigator and pilot exchange heading info', times to turn and usual nav' chatter.

'Coffee time — by now lukewarm from the big black thermos jug. Then mealtime — what a sensation when the steak was started or whatever the galley provided for the flight. Grapefruit juice that tasted like vinegar. And fruit cocktail, apples and oranges. Paper plates and canned cream corn.

'Check on the tip tanks — transfer them both into the mains and when the mains get down far enough, transfer the bomb-bay fuel up to the mains. And watch those sight gauges to make sure you transferred evenly. Keep up the log of all the instrument readings.

'And as the hours wear on, sometimes drowsiness creeps in — you find yourself nodding. Finally, we have reached seven hours out and Nav' says the new heading. We are lighter now and can pull back on the power a bit. Speed has picked up to about 155kts and the recips are pulled down to 2,000 and 29in

'Dawn has now turned into day and day into bright sunlight, making you squint at everything. All the while there is the knowledge that somewhere out there are hostile ships, planes, subs, whatever. And we had better see them FIRST or take the consequences.

'It happens — a Betty zips right under us — a fast 180 and the turrets pound away with tracers all over the place. And those orange balls of light from the Betty aren't Aldis lamp messages — they are honest attempts to seek us out before we hit him. But bow and deck turret get them in there and the crimson starts from the Betty's engine and in a twinkling its gone into the sea.

'When you get back, flight surgeon meets the plane and has brandy for all hands — I don't drink and stow another small bottle in my parachute bag. I'll give them to my squadron leading chief for disposition one day.'

Nosing Around

There can be few, if any, World War 2 aircraft that had a greater number of different nose shapes than the Liberator. Many of these resulted from modifications made to meet the various specialised roles in which Liberators were employed. Others stemmed from attempts to overcome the type's deficiencies in the nose section; poor armament and restricted crew space. Any solution to one invariably conflicted with the other. Never being resolved to the satisfaction of all operators, each tended to pursue its own policy on what was best for their duties. At one point the British were seriously considering the possibility of obtaining detachable nose sections, although this was also because when damaged, noses took so long to repair. These photographs illustrate many but far from all of the different Liberator proboscides.

76
Liberator I (AM259) for transport duties with 'greenhouse' partly painted.

76

77
Liberator I (AM910) with Coastal Command ASV aerial.

78
Liberator II (AL578) transport with sealed nosepiece, doped and plated.

79
Scottish Aviation special nose cone fashioned for transport Liberator II. (AL557, later SX-DAA of Hellenic Airways)

77

ΕΛΛΑΣ
ΚΟΡΗ ΤΩΝ ΑΘΗΝΩΝ
MAID OF ATHENS

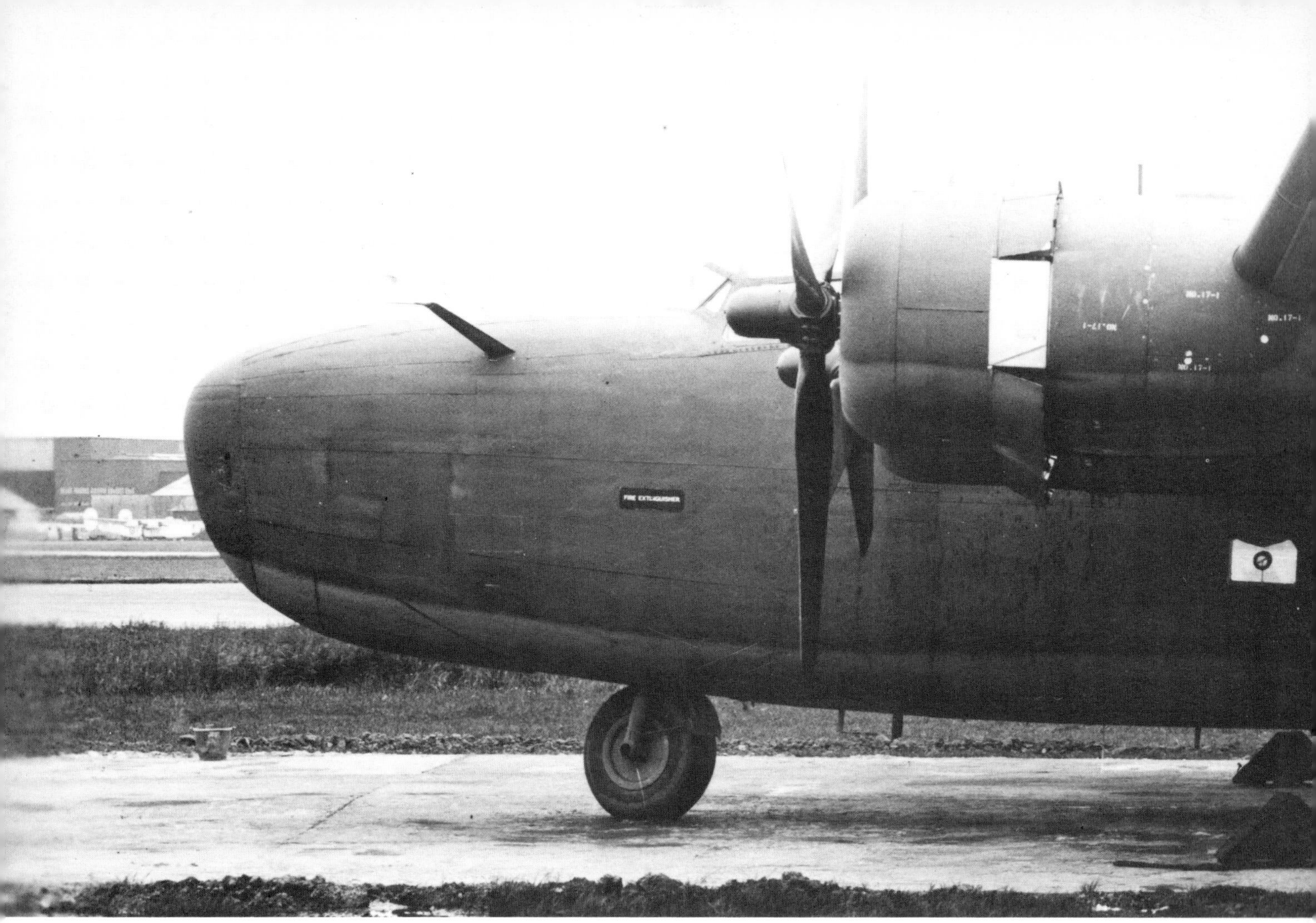

80

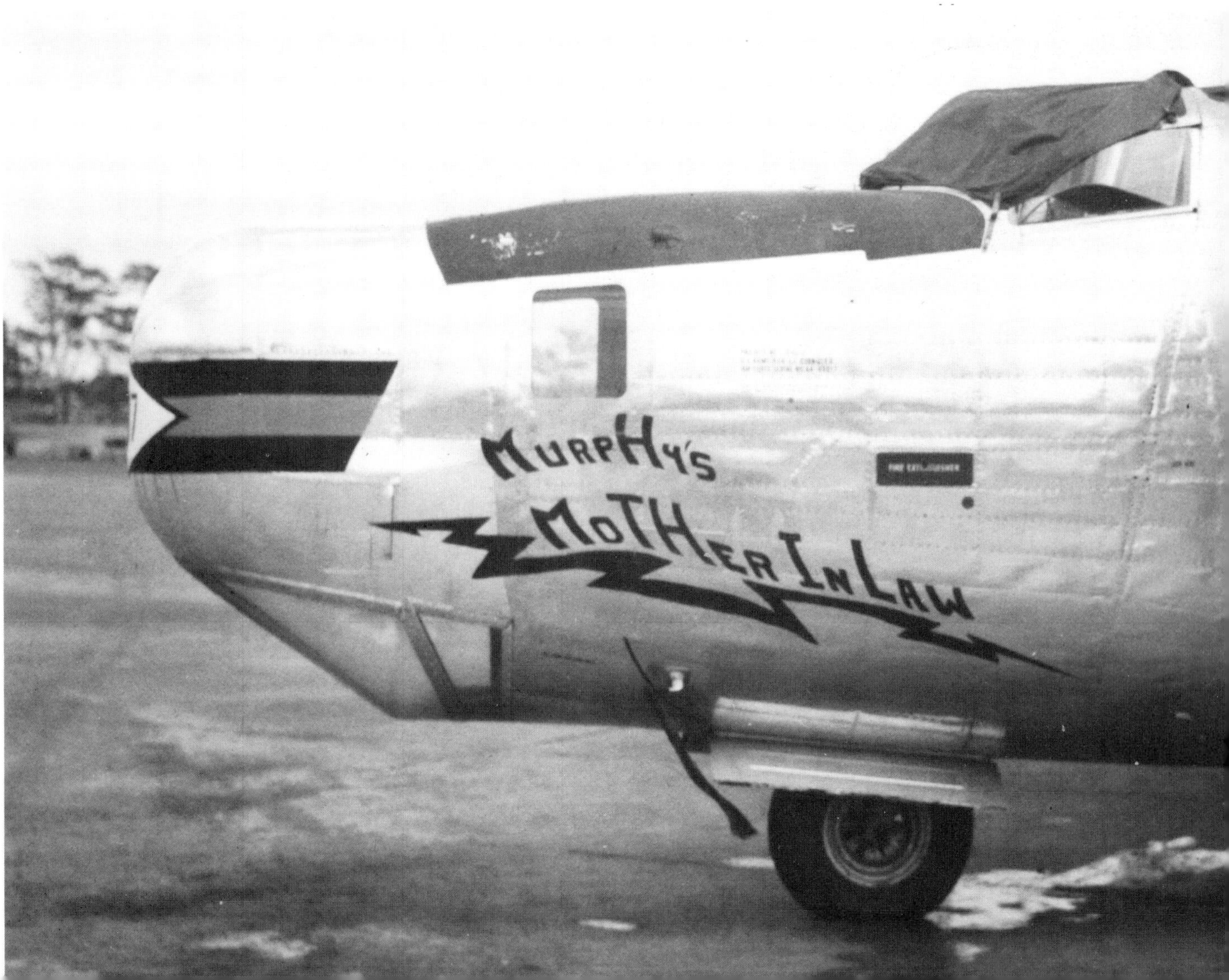

81

82

80
Factory transport nose of C-87. This one belonged to RAF's Liberator C VII, EW615

81
C-109 tanker nose. On the Hump run to India, June 1945, *Murphy's Mother-in-Law*, 44-49017, was formerly a B-24L. C-109 had fuselage tankage for 2,036 US gallons. *via M. Bailey*

82
Standard B-24D nose with field installation of forward firing twin .50in guns. (Aircraft was 42-63962.)

83
B-24D with Convair tail turret transplanted in the nose. A modification carried out by the Hawaiian Air Depot on 42-40144 of 307 BG. *via M. Bailey*

84
B-24D with Oklahoma City Modification Center tail turret graft in the nose. This featured large viewing windows for the bombardier and a distinctive downward thrust to the under line of the nose. *via M. Bailey*

83

84

85
Liberator GR V (B-24D BZ830 of 160 Squadron RAF) with Dumbo nose. The radome housed a centermetric radar scanner.

86
Standard Emerson A-15 model nose turret on a B-24H (42-52086 of 490th BG). This eventually became the preferred type for all B-24 production.

87
Consolidated A-6B turret featured on the majority of B-24J production. It was considered more cramped than the Emerson.

88
Enlarged observation windows for the navigator were a feature of B-24L and B-24M noses. This aircraft also has a revised cockpit canopy for improved pilot outlook *Ford*

89
Erco 250 SH model turret in the PB4Y-2 was quite distinctive. *via M. Bailey*

90
15th Air Force leadship nose where a B-24G nose turret was replaced with a single hand-operated gun and more windows to improve visibility for navigating.

85

86

87

I FIRST TO DEFEAT JAPS IN SWPA (AT BUNA)
I LONGEST IN COMBAT OF US FORCES
I PIERCED EVERY LINE FACED IN TWO WARS
"THE RED ARROW"
32
DIVISION
451757

88

89

90

91
8th Air Force leadship modification with turret removed and improved visibility for bombardier and navigator. A Bell power-boost gun turret assembly from the tail of a B-26 was installed in the lower part of the nose. *via M. Bailey*

92
Special nose used on night flying Carpetbagger B-24s of 859th Bomb Squadron for dropping supplies and agents to patriots in occupied countries. (Aircraft is B-24J 42-50682.)
via S. Blandin

93
Another special fitted to a B-24J used for weather reconnaissance in England. Recording instrumentation attached to the outside of the nose.
via H. Holmes

94
Turretless B-24J (42-100052) used for training with simple nose faring. *W. Larkins*

91

92

93

94

95
Remotely controlled two-gun ball turret on B-24G 42-78399 was part of the development programme for the B-24N. It was a dubious improvement on existing B-24 bomber nose arrangements.

96
Another attempt to improve nose accommodation and outlook was this experimental graft of a B-17G nose to B-24J 42-73130.

97
Yet another featured a lengthened nose and Bendix chin turret. Installed on B-24J 44-40848, pilot visibility suffered considerably.

98
Specially modified RB-24L (44-49630) for training Superfortress gunners. Note barbette under nose. *W. Larkins*

95

96

98

Tail Ends

While not as varied as noses, the other extremity of the Liberator's fuselage did come in several sorts and shapes. Of all defensive positions that at the tail was of major importance as attacking fighters mostly approached from the rear. Early Liberators lacked adequate tail defence and a power turret was considered imperative. But the rear power turret was a mixed blessing as, being heavy, it had an adverse effect on flight characteristics, particularly at high altitudes. Both production and field modification installations of lighter hand-operated gun arrangements were made to help rectify matters.

99

101

99
Liberator I and B-24A had slide back flexing doors to expose a tail gun position. AM922 was delivered without weapons to site there. *IWM*

100
A single .50in calibre hand manipulated machine gun was installed in the USAAF's few B-24As. Assistant radio operator T/Sgt Jack Early doubled as tail gunner on this ATC aircraft, 40-2375.

101
Liberator II had a deeper rear fuselage to take a power turret, but they too were delivered without armament. Sliding windows sealed the tail gunner's position. (Aircraft is AL574.)

102
Twin .50in calibre Brownings mounted in Liberator IIs and LB-30s proved unsatisfactory without some form of damping. When fired they would immediately elevate. *IWM*

100

102

103
Two .30in guns on a tripod proved more practical. Sgt G. Challen manned those in AL574. *via M. Bailey*

104
Boulton & Paul power turrets with four .303in Brownings were installed in Liberator IIs in the UK. Flt Sgt Bill Gunn, RNZAF, has this one at maximum traverse. *J. Musgrave*

105
Boulton & Paul turrets with four .303in guns were also fitted to several Liberator IIIs and Vs (B-24Ds) in place of the original Consolidated rear turret. *via M. Bailey*

106
The Consolidated A-6 with two .50in guns was the standard power turret series fitted to most Liberators during manufacture. The type is displayed here by a B-24J of 450th Bomb Group. *via M. Bailey*

107
A lighter turret, the M-6A, with hand manipulated but hydraulically boosted and damped .50in guns was an alternative factory installation on B-24s during the last nine months of the war.

108
To improve B-24 handling qualities, the Hawaiian Air Depot removed tail turrets and fashioned an open installation with a single hand-held .50in gun on some aircraft. This one is a B-24J of 494th Bomb Group. *via M. Bailey*

109
Extra firepower against attacking jet fighters was the reason for this experimental 8th Air Force installation of a rocket launching tube cluster that could be reloaded from the fuselage hatch above on B-24J 42-50250.

110
Special power-boost lightweight turret of the XB-24N.

103

104

105

106

107

108

109

110

Facts And Fictions

111
The nose wheel was the most troublesome part of the B-24's undercarriage. That on 455th BG's *Dazzlin' Duchess* angled and jammed during retraction and could not be budged. Lt Roy Schott ordered his crew into the rear of the aircraft as he made his approach to land at a 15th Air Force base so that on touch-down the bomber would tip back and drag its rear fuselage. Apart from buckling the underskin This B-24H, 42-64500, was little damaged. *via M. Bailey*

112
Seconds to live. A flak hit under the bomb bay ignited the fuel tanks of this 460th Bomb Group B-24H (41-29508). One crew member has pulled himself out of the forward hatch just behind the cockpit.

113
Another 15th Air Force B-24 with fuel tanks ablaze viewed from a 464th Bomb Group aircraft. (Aircraft K is B-24H 42-52537.) *IWM*

114
German Luftwaffe gun camera film held this B-24 with main tanks erupting in flame during a head-on attack by FW 190s on the 453rd Bomb Group. Other FW190s can be seen banking away from their pass.

115
Despite a massive wound caused by a direct flak hit, the fuselage of this Liberator held together. An 88mm shell detonated inside the waist and blasted away an estimated 12ft of the upper fuselage. Control cables were probably severed as surviving members of the crew baled out. The incident occurred over Weiner Neustadt, Austria on 2 November 1943 and involved a 98th BG B-24D.

For the majority of men who flew in the Liberator it was a reliable, efficient warplane deserving of their loyalty; but there were also many who viewed it with apprehension because of an unnerving experience or from what they had heard. Some of the barrack room beliefs were justified; but most were not.

During 1942-43 the B-24 gained a reputation as a 'problem plane' at the bomber training bases conducted by the 2nd Air Force in western United States. In 1943 alone, 850 2nd Air Force crewmen were killed in 298 B-24 accidents, the precise cause in many cases never being established. A spate of crashes at Alamogordo, New Mexico, led Brigadier General Nathan Forrest to report: 'The people down here are scared to death of their airplanes and it is very bad.' Major factors in this unfortunate situation were expediency and inexperience. Better trained mechanics, a less forced flying programme and a greater understanding of the B-24's foibles, helped reduce the accident rate in subsequent months; but the damage was done, like the Martin B-26 and Lockheed P-38, the B-24 was rumoured 'a killer' amongst trainees, a reputation that would linger and occasionally be given some substance in combat theatres.

An oft repeated belief was that a B-24 would crash if an engine failed on take-off. The maximum approved all-up weight for a B-24J, the heaviest model in the development chain, was 62,000lb, with a recommendation that it be no more than 56,000lb for inexperienced pilots. However, in combat theatres, particularly where high-altitude bombing was practised, B-24s regularly grossed 65,000lb and sometimes a gross overload of 71,000lb. The combined power of the four Pratt & Whitney Twin Wasps, 4,800hp, would lift such loads, but understandably if an engine failed at a critical point the situation could indeed be perilous. Nevertheless, heavily loaded B-24s did survive such failures for the crashes were not so much due to lack of power but the characteristics of the Davis wing. When an outboard engine failed, the wing on that side dropped suddenly. If the pilots could immediately bring the trim tab up on the other wing to arrest the drop and apply full rudder tab to maintain directional stability loss of control could be averted. The trim tabs, designed with low gearing actuation for fine adjustment, could only be brought into the full countering position by several revolutions of their control wheel with a possibly fatal time delay. In later Liberators modifications allowed an

111

112

override on tab adjustment for emergencies requiring full countering.

The Twin Wasp R-1830-43 and 65 model engines were basically sound and probably the most reliable air-cooled radials ever built. So much so that enthusiasts for that other American heavy bomber were known to quip that the engines were the only good things about the B-24. When moderately loaded Liberators could, in favourable circumstances, maintain formation and deliver a bomb load with one propeller feathered. Lightened combat Liberators were known to return on two engines, while it was possible with a quarter fuel load and empty bomb-bay to stay aloft on just one inboard engine, a feat often demonstrated by instructors to apprehensive novice pilots.

It was generally accepted that the B-24 would not endure the battle damage that a B-17 could. This was endorsed by some Luftwaffe pilots who noted that the Liberator would take fire more easily than a Fortress. There is no statistical evidence to support this, but the concentration of fuel tanks around the wing centre section over the bomb-bay certainly increased the danger of destruction if fire started in that area. B-17s were known to survive a complete burn-out of a main tank (positioned in the wing clear of the fuselage); a B-24 never.

There is photographic evidence that Liberators could suffer considerable damage to their fuselages and return to base for a safe landing. Severe damage to wings or empennage was another matter. If this was sustained by aircraft heavily laden, or at high altitude, the pilots had difficulty in maintaining level flight. Control pressures were normally rated as heavy, and in such circumstances they could become more than the pilots could handle. There were instances where B-24s had the tailplane on one side of

113

114 115

116

the aircraft completely severed by enemy action or accident yet both pilots, by extreme physical effort, were able to keep the aircraft in level flight; but to attempt a landing would have been suicidal. With severe wing damage it was sometimes possible to keep control and bring the aircraft down safely for a landing. Probably the most extraordinary example is that involving an RAF Coastal Command Liberator V in the early hours of Christmas Day 1943. Aircraft 'O' of No 224 Squadron was preparing to attack an enemy convoy near the Spanish coast when another aircraft flying above released a flare, brilliantly illuminating 'O' at 4,000ft over the convoy. Immediately the Liberator was subjected to the combined fire of six destroyers and while evasively making a steep left turn the crew heard a large bang. The Liberator lost height rapidly and the pilot, Flt Lt A. R. Laughland, finding it would not respond to the controls pushed the throttles wide open in an endeavour to bring the left wing up. After several anxious seconds the Liberator was brought back on an even keel. One of the crew reported that part of the wing was missing but the pilot found that the aircraft could be flown quite well with full right trim and the control wheel wound over almost one full turn to the right. After jettisoning the bomb load, he made the three hour flight back to England where, still keeping the control wheel hard over to the right and by careful use of engines, Laughland made a perfect night landing at St Eval. To their astonishment the crew discovered that exactly 13ft of the left wing was missing!

116
Although the flap on the right wing was blown completely away this 376th BG B-24J kept flying.

117
The huge wheel well was often a point of wing failure if severe battle damage was sustained in this area.

117

The Liberator's reputation for falling out of high altitude formation if turbulence was encountered was justified to the extent that the aircraft became progressively less stable with a full load above 20,000ft. In such circumstances B-24s occasionally stalled and spun but the frequency has been exaggerated. What was not true was that a B-24 in a spin stood little chance of being brought out. In fact, the Liberator had good stall and spin recovery characteristics. Pilots regained control from quite prolonged spins, even with full bomb loads, which says much for the sound construction of the type. One spectacular occurrence involved a B-24D of 380th Bomb Group at dawn on 26 December 1943. It was one of a force despatched in darkness from a New Guinea base to rendezvous off the coast of New Britain at 10,000ft where, unexpectedly, they came under intense anti-aircraft fire from a shore battery. In the course of taking evasive action two aircraft nearly collided. Lt Harold Mulholland managed to pull his Liberator into a tight climbing turn as the other seemed set to plough into his. The next moment Mulholland's aircraft stalled, flipped over on its back and went into a near vertical spin. The bomber dropped 7,000ft before the pilots managed to arrest its plunge, a feat needing their combined strengths on the control columns. The shaken crew reported the B-24 had developed a distinct dihedral and as control was difficult Mulholland abandoned the mission and made for the nearest Allied airstrip. A safe landing was made despite control problems and the eight 1,000lb bombs still in the bay. Both wings outboard of the engines were warped and bent up.

That the top turret broke loose in hard crash-landings and crushed the pilots was not only a well-aired belief with B-24 aircrew, but the subject of many 'Unsatisfactory Reports' passed to higher authorities. This was particularly so with the nose turret models where the nose tended to crumple on contact with the ground causing sharp deceleration which was believed to break the top turret from its mounts. It was even more evident in a large number of incidents where a Liberator suffered nose wheel collapse on landing, when the nose ploughed into the runway, with pilots and others on the flight deck then being crushed by the top turret. Although 'Unsatisfactory Reports' on this matter had been submitted for many months, it was not until the spring of 1945 that a serious investigation was undertaken. Experiments showed that the turret did not break loose in these circumstances. From examination of photographs showing B-24s wrecked in crashes, Wright Field engineers could find no evidence to support dislodgement. Therefore, two old B-24s were obtained for structural tests in the Special Static Test Building where the first of these was conducted on 21 June 1945. The top turret and supporting structure were subjected to combined forward and downward loads, the test being discontinued when the turret armour plate pulled off at forces equivalent to 11.4g forward and 2.14g downward decelerations, but there was no failure of turret of support structure.

118
Needing the strength of both pilots to deal with the enormous control pressures, this 392nd Bomb Group B-24H was flown back to England after a bomb severed the left tail stabiliser. As a landing was not possible the crew managed to parachute to safety.

119
Harold Mulholland's B-24 in its vertical plunge near Cape Gloucester. Recorded by a photographer in the waist of another 380th Bomb Group B-24 flying at 9,500ft. *Liberator Club*

118

119

A more exacting test was set up and carried out on 12 July in which one aircraft was subjected to a simulated nose-down, main wheel only crash-landing. Straps were riveted to the underside of the forward fuselage for a test load to pull aft, simulating the retardation forces of friction developing as the forward fuselage slithered along the runway. Forward pulling loads by hydraulic actuators were applied to the inboard engine mounts and main landing gear struts. Bags of lead shot were distributed about the structure to give the desired gross weight. Forces beyond the design ultimate load were applied before the fuselage failed in compression between the cockpit and the turret. Continued application of load caused the tail of the aircraft to swing upwards, folding cockpit and turret into one another to a point where the latter would have crushed any occupants of the former. The turret structure remained firm through the test proving, as far as Wright Field was concerned, that the fuselage not the turret was the problem. There were plans to strengthen the fuselage in this area so that in a crash failure would occur elsewhere, but the cessation of hostilities saw this work abandoned.

On a smooth surface it was possible to make wheels-up landings with Liberators that did little damage to the fuselage and allowed speedy repair. Often such landings were accomplished without bending a single propeller blade. It depended, as did the outcome of so many emergencies, upon the skill of the pilot.

Little chance of crew survival in a water landing was one area where hear-say was not far from reality. The poor ditching characteristics of the Liberator were subject to investigation both in the United States and Britain but there was no really satisfactory solution other than a major re-design of the whole fuselage. In operational theatres strengthening supports were devised which took the form of bearers that could be quickly installed if a water landing was imminent. Later production B-24s had four such bomb-bay stiffeners as standard equipment and it is probable that they helped with the slightly improved numbers that escaped from successful ditching.

A rumour which must have been started by B-17 advocates was that anyone selected for pilot training in B-24s had to weigh not less than 200lb and was sent on a special muscle building course. This, naturally, was pure fantasy as many of the most honoured and successful Liberator pilots were quite diminutive. Although all who flew high altitude operations will concur that it was no place for a weakling.

120
The result of a heavy crash landing. Due to a switching problem the 487th Bomb Group B-24H, 42-52581, suffered failure of all four engines while over its base. The co-pilot and engineer were killed by the top turret.

121
B-24D 41-23650 at the start of the 12 July 1945 test. Rods attached to engine mounts and main undercarriage are under tension. Cables fixed to the underside of the nose and the hydraulic rams supplying the muscle are also visible.
R. Cavanagh

122
Conclusion of test showing fuselage fracture and turret mechanism crushing cockpit.
via R. Cavanagh

120

Keeping Her Flying

Howard Hill

'A B-24 was a lot of airplane. Regular maintenance as specified by the technical orders called for a lot of man hours and the people who wrote those up didn't allow for the extra problems experienced at a combat station. There was no such thing as a shift; if your plane wanted work on it then you stayed until the job was done. Sometimes this meant working right through the night. There was no shelter from rain or cold, and all you could do was dress warm. We were young — I guess the average age of a mechanic was under 25 — so we took the English weather in our stride, even if we continually bitched about it. It was constant go, go, go; seemed that someone was always saying we need that airplane ready by such and such an hour. And you worked at it because you knew that if you didn't have things perfect you could endanger the lives of the crew who would be flying her. They had enough dangers without you adding to them.

'I was a crew chief which meant I had a B-24 to maintain and three men to help me. The last thing you wanted was for your plane to abort a mission because of a mechanical failure. The combat crew didn't thank you if they had to turn back half way to a target; it meant they had an extra period of pre-combat tension to face in finishing their tour. Group didn't like it as it was one less plane bombing the enemy. An abort was something of a black mark against a crew chief. So you did your best to see it never happened to your plane; I guess it was a matter of personal pride as well.

'Aeronautical design and engineering at this time had not really advanced to a high state of reliability and a lot of things could go wrong. You had to check, check and check again. The abort rate for my group, the 458th, was around 22% of B-24s scheduled for a mission, which is pretty high. The 8th Air Force average was about 15%. Often it wasn't the ground crew's fault as components would fail or the pilots might overstrain the power plants.

'I can't say the B-24 had any major maintenance problems or mechanical weaknesses. It was a rugged and well engineered plane for

123
For routine maintenance the cowlings round the R-1830 radials hinged up and did not have to be completely detached and laboriously lifted down to and up from the ground. Note open life raft hatch on this Liberator II of No 159 Squadron and the two 'erks' out on the far wing tip having a quiet fag away from fuel fumes. The Mark II was the only model Liberator to use Curtiss Electric propellers.
J. Musgrave.

123

124

125

124
B-24 plug changing and prop' adjustment had to be carried out a long way from terra firma. Even with the necessary stands and ladders footholds could be precarious — as in the case of the man working on the inboard side of No 1. Several mechanics were seriously injured by tumbles on to the concrete and a few killed. Taken at Hardwick, England, this photograph proves that the Middle East, South East Asia and Pacific were not the only war zones where mechanics had to sweat on the job. *via Archer*

125
Spraying anti-freeze solution over the wings of an RAF Coastal Command Liberator on a frosty November day. If needs be this was repeated every three hours to ensure safety at take-off. Note Leigh Light (under the right wing) for illuminating vessels during darkness. *Flight*

126
Polish mechanics work on a Liberator VI that came back from 'ops' with No 2 out and the 'prop' feathered. An aircraft of No 301 Squadron manned by Poles and operating from Italy over eastern Europe delivering supplies and agents. The countries visited during these sorties are recorded with national flag symbols on the nose. *Polish Official*

its day. If I was to single out one thing that was a regular problem it would be the electrical generators. Generator drive shafts were always snapping off. We had a bugaboo about this. It caused a lot of planes to abort.

'The engines were pretty hardy although they were under a lot of strain at high altitude. A tell-tale sign of internal trouble was metal filings in the sump oil, so you checked that regularly. Starters sometimes failed at pre-flight. For some reason the engagement parts weren't strong enough to turn a cold engine over. It was farily easy to work round the engines as the cowlings folded up out of the way and didn't have to be struggled up and down from the ground as with a B-17. My crew and I usually made engine changes when necessary. The engineering people brought the new ones to us ready to install as a pack with accessories fitted. There were four main bolts that secured the engine to the nacelle and most of the time was taken up with connecting pipes and wiring. We had to take great care not to damage the delicate tubing for the fire extinguisher system that ran around the top of the cylinder and could be easily squashed. Engine life could be just a few hours or many hundreds.; I guess I changed about a dozen on my B-24s. The turbo superchargers didn't ever cause me much trouble except when they had taken a piece of flak. When this happened, as they spun at such a high speed the whole compeller tore apart and the fragments slashed into the wing and fuselage.

'Many maintenance and repair jobs could not be done out on the revetments and the plane would be taken to the hangar where a special engineering crew would work on it. One such task was replacing the fuel cells if they had been badly shot up. This was a very difficult job as the tanks were heavy and there was little space to work in the wing.

'The B-24 always seemed to have fuel leaks around the bomb-bay area where many of the fuel lines passed through. No one smoked near the bomb-bay and armourers had to be especially careful when loading bombs not to cause sparks. The bombs, armament, oxygen and fuel were always loaded by special teams. They could get quite lax — they did the same job day after day and night after night — and it was always my policy to have someone close at hand to see that nothing was damaged. The bomb-bay had a lot of equipment that could easily get damaged.

'The B-24 hydraulics were good but if it did happen to get air in the system then, oh boy, you were in for a long, difficult job bleeding it out. The undercarriage stood up to normal landings well but if it was put down hard and ran off the runway into the rough something usually gave or twisted. Very rarely could you tow them back to the revetment. Although a B-24 main wheel stood nearly 5ft high they were relatively easy to change as the jacking equipment provided was very good. We had a lot of trouble

with tyres being cut by the clips from the 50-calibre gun belts that had fallen out of planes on to the runway. Precautions were taken to prevent this but it still occurred. Most tyres didn't see the tread out but were removed because of cuts or some other problem that might have led to a blow-out.

'To support each ground crew there were teams for most specialist work such as flight electrics, flak patching, turret mechanisms and the like. Additionally, we mechanics tended to become interested in particular items. I liked carburettors and if some other crew chief had a problem he couldn't solve then he would come to me. Likewise I would go to another ground crew if they had a man who had special knowledge that could help me. We had 63 ground crew men in our squadron, the 752nd, and we could turn our hands to most anything if the need arose.

'The revetments (hardstands) on our airfield were built to accommodate one heavy bomber apiece. As there weren't enough for every B-24 in the group two bombers were usually parked on each. This was no great problem except when your buddy was winding his airplane up, tail towards you. The slip stream generated by these four fans blew you and your equipment all over the place. I've seen my tool box go flying.

'Except in an emergency — shortage of mechanics or the arrival of extra aircraft — a crew chief in our group only had one aircraft in his charge. My first was '669' which mushroomed into the ground at the end of the base on return from the 458th's first mission. Seven of the crew were killed. The replacement was a B-24H named *Final Approach* — the 'final approach' in view being the USA. Several crews flew her and she gathered her share of flak damage. Her record was good and with no aborts she was often the plane visiting Brass from Wing or Division HQ chose to ride. Sometimes they left their staff cars unattended while they were gone on the mission. As they'd taken my plane I figured I had a right to use their staff car and on one occasion we used it to visit a local pub. Nobody questioned us and if the Brass noticed that the car had been moved when they returned they never said anything.

'In February 1945 *Final Approach* had more missions on it than any other B-24 in our group and in early March she passed 100, still without an abort. Thirteen was her unlucky number because on mission 113 she finally aborted. She continued to lead the group in missions flown and had passed 120 when on 9 April she didn't come back. Over Lechfeld accurate flak had fired No 2 engine. The flames couldn't be extinguished and several members of the crew parachuted. *Final Approach* was seen to explode when down to about 5,000ft. It was a tough thing to take after sweating out for all those missions: Left me with a sort of empty feeling. No other plane in the Group had a record to match.'

127
Some wounded GIs were retrained for USAAF ground tasks. At a rehabilitation centre in England the fuselage of B-24J 42-110140 served as a 'flak patching' trainer. This aircraft had brief service with 491st Bomb Group before being written off as beyond repair.

Vulnerable But Lucky

Peter Massare

Most difficult and dangerous of Liberator combat operations were the high altitude, close formation, daylight missions conducted by the USAAF over Europe. Initially the major establishment was to have been with the 8th Air Force in England, but in the autumn of 1943 the USAAF decided to divert nearly half the new heavy bomber units earmarked for the 8th to southern Italy for incorporation in a new strategic bombing arm, the 15th Air Force. Fifteen of the 21 bomber groups that ultimately made up the 15th were B-24 equipped.

Generally overshadowed by the older, larger 8th Air Force, the 15th nevertheless grew from 'a pretty disorganised mob' — as the senior Allied air commander in the Mediterranean observed — to become a performer of consistently efficient bombing operations. This expertise was developed in the face of formidable opposition particularly during the first half of 1944. In fact, 15th Air Force B-24s incurred the highest average loss per sortie ratio for any Liberator force during this period. One of the most battered yet resilient units was the 451st Bomb Group which in 216 missions lost 135 B-24s. It was also the only group in the 15th Air Force to earn three Distinguished Unit Citations, each for a specific bombing mission. Peter Massare was a B-24 pilot who participated in several of the 451st's battles. This is his story of war in the Liberators:

'My initial introduction to B-24s, in the summer of 1943, was a sour one. No one qualifying as a pilot wanted to fly a B-24; at that particular time *the* four-engine bomber was the B-17. Having flown twin-engine aircraft in advanced training I had figured I was going to fly P-38s, which is what I wanted to fly; a fighter. If not that then the A-20 Havoc or B-25 Mitchell, speedy twin-engine light and medium bombers. I didn't know anything about B-24s until I was sent to Gowen Field, Idaho, and discovered all they had was B-24s! Neither did it take me long to find out the B-24 only had derogatory nicknames — like "Flying Coffin", "Flying Boxcar", "The Crate the B-17 Came In", and the like. It looked ugly and was very much of a disappointment as far as my initial impression went. I heard a lot of bad things about the B-24 but an awful lot turned out not to be true.

'Having been checked out in the aircraft I was assigned to the 727th Bomb Squadron of the 451st Group, which was training at Fairmont, Nebraska, to go overseas. The training was intensive; seemed we worked 24hrs a day, but we had few mishaps with the airplanes. One bit of excitement was when Captain Kendall Young, my operations

128

128
Captain Peter Massare.

129

129
Little Butch, B-24H 42-7765, after its take-off crash. The fuselage was slashed just behind the pilot's position by the propeller of No 2 engine. The navigator, who was on the flight deck, was seriously injured.
P. Massare

officer, couldn't get the nose wheel to lock down for landing. He finally solved this by hitting the runway hard with his main wheels so the shock shook the nose wheel into the locked position. In training the problems we had were not with the aircraft but with the men, getting them familiar with all aspects of the job. Average age of a pilot was about 21 and by the time we were considered ready to move overseas he would have had about 250 hours on the B-24, which wasn't a lot of experience to be handling such a complex piece of equipment.

'The Group flew the South Atlantic to Africa and arrived at Gioia del Colle air base in Italy in January 1944 to become part of the 15th Air Force. My squadron, for which I acted as assistant operations officer, flew its first mission on the 30th, an attack on a radar station at Fier, Albania. Such missions over Italy were, I soon discovered, comparatively easy in contrast to the raids into Southern Germany, Austria and Romania which I was soon to experience. At first there was an unlimited number of missions to be flown until your flight surgeon determined you were unable to continue. Then they changed it to a 50 mission tour and soon modified this so that a "hard target" would count as two missions towards your total. The "hard targets" were anything in Germany or Austria and distant places like Ploesti or Bucharest in the Balkans. The Italian targets only counted one mission. In all I flew 39 sorties to rack up my 50 mission tour.

'Our squadron suffered very heavy losses. The attrition rate was something the individual could only guess but I would think it averaged about 33%. What would happen was that over a milk run target there would be few, if any, losses while at places like Ploesti, Vienna and Munich the loss factor would often be 50%. On our first raid to Ploesti, 5 April, the 727th lost four out of seven sent and that's more than 50%. Fighters were the chief cause of losses during the first four months of operations; after that they still occasionally hit us hard until the late summer. The last time was on 23 August when we were going to Markersdorf airfield at Vienna. Wave after wave came at us out of clouds and knocked down nine of our 24 B-24s. I understand that was the last major attack by enemy fighters on a 15th Air Force formation.

'In contrast to training, the B-24s we were flying in combat were often loaded to capacity and that gave us problems. What I didn't like was the terrible take-off situation. It was so critical that if you got the plane off the ground you felt you had 50% of the mission flown. It seemed that if the engines spluttered just a little bit the possibility of getting off the ground was nil. Many B-24s crashed off the end of the runway and when this happened they invariably burst into flames and blew up. My best friend was killed this way. Some crashes may have been caused by poor base conditions in the early days as the engineers hadn't got things perfect and we sometimes had to run through puddles of water. Also, when summer came and the dirt taxiways dried out aircraft would throw up clouds of dust, particularly when waiting to take off and alternately idling engines and then running them up to keep the spark plugs from carbonising. A lot of this dust would get into the air filters and you just hoped it didn't choke them. On our permanent base at Castelluccio the runway was steel plank and a mile long. The form was to hold the plane down until the co-pilot called out 120mph before lifting off; then get the gear up in a hurry so that we had better airflow and the speed would pick up right away. We had an advantage in that our field was on a plateau and after take-off you could

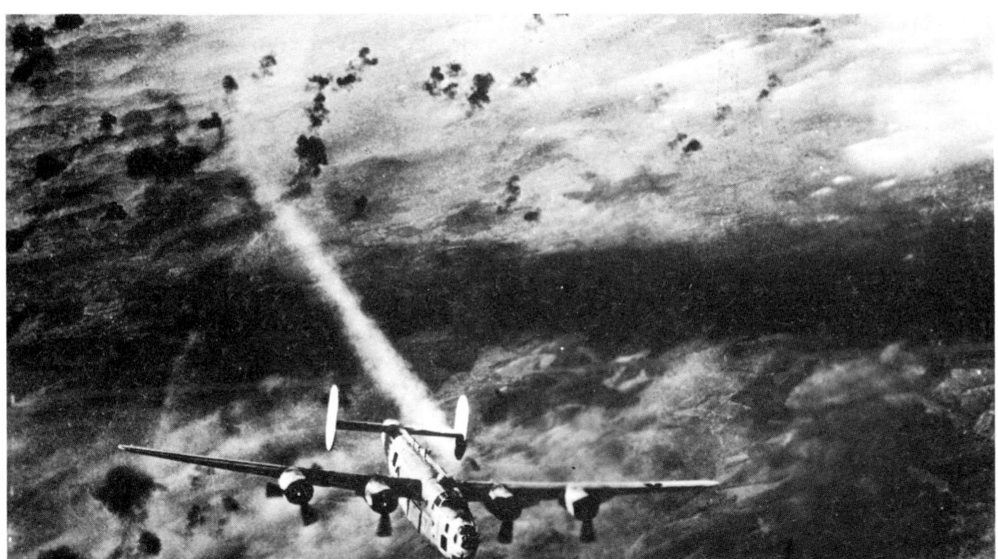

130

130
A limping 451st Bomb Group Liberator comes through Vienna's flak.

swoop down a little into the valley beyond to pick up speed.

'On one mission I was taking-off in a B-24 called *Little Butch* and had just touched 90mph when the left tyre blew. We tried applying right brake and cutting power of Nos 3 and 4 in an effort to keep the plane on the runway, but it started shuddering like crazy, the nose wheel crumpled and in we went. It was the first occasion on our base that a take-off accident hadn't ended in fire and explosion. My bombardier was struck in the head and seriously injured by a blade of No 2 propeller. The rest of us were very lucky to get out alive. I received severe back injuries in jumping from the top hatch and striking a piece of wreckage.

'A fully laden B-24 with gas, bombs, ammunition and personnel was one loggy airplane. It had a very slow rate of climb and took a long while to reach the 20,000ft or more required for operations. It flew well and handled well at low altitudes but the higher you climbed the harder it became to anticipate the controls. Beyond 23,000ft a fully laden B-24 was very sluggish and floundered. Because of the hesitancy on the controls it could be dangerous to try and fly close formation. B-24 formations were never as tight as those of B-17s at high altitude. Normal heavy bomber formations were flown with a lead flight of six aircraft flanked by another flight of six at high right and another at low left to make a combat box. Another box at different altitude made up the whole 36 plane group formation. For safety it had to be a loose formation at very high altitudes because of the control problems. Most air collisions were caused by the swinging back and forth that occurred in the thin air. If you were down to, say, 10,000ft you could tuck a wing in back of another person's wing and fly a stable, tight formation as well as could be done with a B-17 or any other type of airplane.

'Mechanically the B-24 was very sound. It was well made and very reliable. The Pratt & Whitney engines were probably the best radials of the war. They were superior to the Wrights of the B-17 that threw oil all over the place, and the B-29s which had a tendency to over-heat on take-off. The two problems we had were common to other engines. Magneto failure was one; they required constant attention and the fuses changed. The other was turbo-superchargers which really had to be watched. If one went out while at high altitude the power loss would soon have you straggling — and a straggler didn't last long when fighters were about. Oxygen leaks were a frequent trouble; again this was not something peculiar to the B-24 but due to the stage of oxygen system technology at that time. Oxygen was essential at the altitudes we operated and a failure could mean aborting a mission. I personally had this problem on a sortie to Bucharest. What I chose to do was have the engineer give me a walk-around emergency bottle very 15min — which was about as long as they lasted — and this way we didn't have to leave the formation. On the same mission the turbo on No 2 engine gave trouble so part of our bomb load was jettisoned to allow us to keep with the group all the way to the target and back.

'Safety was always uppermost in our minds and we used a cockpit check list. It had 24 items to check before starting engines, 10 for starting engines, nine before taxying and 18 before and seven after take-off. The same for landing; 18 times before, four after and seven to secure the airplane. Also, before and after flight we would go

131
The 727th Bomb Squadron leaves the flak and fires at Ploesti. *P. Massare*

132
A 724th Bomb Squadron B-24M unloads framentation bombs. Unlike the 8th Air Force, 15th Air Force retained the ball turrets on its Liberators to the end of hostilities. When lowered, the turret's drag reduced airspeed by some 10mph. *P. Massare*

133

round the airplane with the crew chief. If you wanted to live you didn't slack on that. The ground crews had a hard, tiring job keeping the B-24s in commission and they did excellent work.

'In our group we flew with a crew of 10; pilot, co-pilot, bombardier, navigator and six enlisted men, engineer, assistant engineer, radio operator, assistant radio operator, tail gunner and belly gunner. The two assistants doubled as gunners in the waist. In the summer of 1944 it became policy for only the lead and deputy lead aircraft in each flight to carry a bombardier who was dropped from the other crews, their bombs being toggled by the navigator when he saw those from the lead plane drop.

'In my opinion the B-24 was far too vulnerable for the kind of war we were fighting. Although by the end of the war the Group's gunners had claimed nearly a hundred of the enemy fighters that attacked, the B-24 was no match for the heavily armed and armoured German fighters who, because of the loose formations we flew, did not meet the concentrated defensive fire they should

133
Patches, a 726th Bomb Squadron B-24G, over the Alps. This natural barrier prevented many ailing 15th Air Force bombers from regaining their bases. *P. Massare*

134
Mud seeped through the PSP runways in winter and every take-off spattered the under fuselage and tail. *Calamity Jane*, B-24H 42-52440 'A' of 727th Bomb Squadron, displays the evidence. *via M. Bailey*

134

135

135
This B-24 crashed while landing at Pantanella, Italy. In a matter of seconds the ignition of high octane gasolene, oxygen, oil and magnesium produced an inferno. *IWM*

136
North American Aviation production at Dallas featured the B-24G which was externally similar to the H model but incorporated many manufacturing differences. In order to simplify maintenance and logistics the B-24G was, apart from a few wandering examples, consigned only to the 15th Air Force as a combat aircraft. This example served 737th Bomb Squadron, 454th Bomb Group. *via M. Bailey*

136

have done. Murderous as some of the fighter attacks on our formations were, flak was far more frightening to endure. As the Russians advanced and the German perimeter contracted so they were able to build up the concentrations of guns at targets like Vienna.

'At the end of October 1944 I had finished my war in a B-24 and was sent home. Some of my crew were not so fortunate; my nose gunner was mortally wounded by flak in his head. A tail gunner was also wounded by flak but was able to return to flying after three or four weeks. There had also been occasions the airplane was so shot up I thought we would never make it back. Once over Munich we had a near flak hit that riddled fuselage and wings with splinters and things looked bad. The only major damage was to the hydraulics and we used the emergency system to get the wheels lowered — we made it down safely even though we only had one shot at the brakes before the fluid was exhausted.

'What I saw from the cockpit of a B-24 was an awful lot of other people being killed and other B-24s going down. It was a tough thing to take, particularly if they were friends of yours. There was Mike Boyle. Over Ploesti on 5 May his aircraft took direct hits and caught fire. Although flames were sweeping out of his escape hatch he kept that B-24 flying level to allow other members of the crew to bale out. At the time we didn't know that his co-pilot had been killed or that Boyle was badly wounded in the legs himself. He kept that thing flying until it finally blew up, losing his own life in saving others. Posthumously he got the Distinguished Service Cross, highest decoration to any man in our Group.

'On the 23 August mission to Vienna I watched horrified as the plane ahead was shot down. I was flying Number 4, in the slot position a little below and directly behind the lead ship. Suddenly a Focke-Wulf appeared directly above my cockpit. He seemed so close I felt I could almost feel up and wipe the oil slick from under his cowl. He must have come in out of the sun for none of my gunners fired a single shot at him. He seemed to hover there as he pumped 20mm shell into the lead ship. The victim dropped away and when about a mile distant floundered and exploded. Not a chute was seen. And there were many other simialr occasions which hardened my opinion that the B-24 was very vulnerable to both flak and fighters.

'Despite several missions which I can only describe as horrific, in my total 273 combat hours in a B-24 I got to like it. I had to like it — I had nothing else to compare it with. It did the job, it got me back and that's the main thing.'

Heroes

The history of the Liberator in combat is studded with incidents of unusual bravery by its crews. It is probable that the most courageous and selfless acts were unrecorded as there were no surviving witnesses. Bravery is a facet of human behaviour of which it is often difficult to make comparative evaluations. How, for example, does the bravery exhibited by such as Lt Cdr Norman Miller, who on several occasions deliberately pitted his lone PB4Y-1 against the defences of Japanese island bases in order to attack shipping, compare to that of a man like Lt Charles Stevens who, after flak had blasted away nose and navigator of his Liberator and stopped two engines, did not abandon the resulting unstable wreck but doggedly nursed it back across the English Channel and crash-landed without further hurt to his crew. Such deeds must have presented problems for those bestowing official recognition of exceptional bravery, although this does not explain why some deeds so obviously deserving of a major award received seemingly minor acknowledgement and vice versa. Many recommendations for the highest decorations were never approved; not, one feels, so much because the candidate was undeserving but rather because of a policy to maintain the exclusiveness of top awards.

The United States bestowed its premier award for deeds of supreme valour on nine Liberator crewmen during the course of hostilities, seven of them posthumously. The sole US Navy Liberator flier to win the Medal of Honor was also involved in the earliest action with a Liberator to earn this highest award. On 6 July 1943, 35-year old Lt Cdr Bruce Van Voorhis, CO of VB-102, attacked the Japanese weather station and seaplane base at Kapingamarangi, a remote atoll near the Solomon Islands. In the face of both fighters and AA fire he made six runs in his lone PB4Y-1 to attack the installation before being shot down into the sea. There were no survivors. Five Medal of Honor awards were made for the famous low-level mission to the Ploesti oil refineries on 1 August 1943. *Hell's Wench*, the B-24D in which Col Addison Baker and his pilot Maj John Jerstad were leading the 93rd Group, was set alight three miles from the target. Rather than jeopardise the formation's attack by turning away and causing confusion, the leaders jettisoned the bomb load and took their burning aircraft over the target before going down. Both men were killed. Two other formation leaders, Col John Kane of the 98th Group in *Hail Columbia* and Col Leon Johnson of the 44th Group in *Suzy Q* also won the award for leadership but both survived. The refinery targets they were detailed to attack were found to have already been bombed by preceding formations and the defences alerted. Both men would have been justified in turning away but both unwaveringly pressed their attacks. The fifth Medal of Honor at Ploesti went to 1-Lt Lloyd Hughes of the 389th Group whose B-24 was hit by ground fire on approach to the target. Despite an opportunity to immediately belly-land in open fields, Hughes chose to try and bomb the target, which he did, only to crash and lose his life.

Action on 5 June 1944, the day prior to the launching of the cross-Channel invasion of the Continent, brought the next Medal of

137

137
Ploesti flak removed a chunk of *Suzy Q's* rudder. A photograph taken as the B-24D carried Colonel Leon Johnson to Africa during the operation that would bring him the Medal of Honor.
W. Cameron

Honor to a Liberator man. Lt-Col Leon Vance, Deputy Commander of the 489th Group, was flying in a 44th Group pathfinder aircraft leading a formation of B-24s in attacking defences on the French coast. The B-24H was hit by flak, the pilot killed and Vance's right foot practically severed. The bomber was brought back to the English coast where Vance, who had received emergency first aid, took the controls and ordered the crew to bale out, knowing he himself had little change of surviving. He was, however, able to ditch the bomber and escape from the wreckage to be picked up by a ship. Sadly, Vance was lost in a hospital evacuation transport aircraft which disappeared near Iceland on 26 July 1944.

Ploesti was again the scene for action that brought another B-24 flier a Medal of Honor. On 9 July 1944 the aircraft flown by Lt Donald Pucket of 98th Group was hit by flak at high altitude over this infamous target. One man was killed and six other members of the crew wounded. Exhibiting remarkable composure Pucket righted the bomber, then passed control to the co-pilot while he helped administer first aid to the wounded. As only two engines were functioning properly, Pucket tried to lighten the aircraft by throwing out loose equipment but it continued to lose height. Pucket then returned to the cockpit and ordered the crew to bale out. Three wounded men could or would not jump so Pucket stayed in the cockpit hoping to make a crash-landing. Before this could be attempted the Liberator had a further engine failure and crashed into a mountain.

A similar act of self sacrifice earned the last Medal of Honor for a B-24 crewman. Maj Horace Carswell of 308th Group was piloting a B-24J on the night of 26 October 1944 looking for enemy shipping in the South China sea. He located a 12-ship Japanese convoy and made a bombing run at low altitude. As the first bombs had missed their target Carswell brought the Liberator in again for another attack, fully realising he had lost the element of surprise. This time direct hits were obtained on a tanker from 500ft but anti-aircraft fire was intense and the bomber was badly damaged. Carswell managed to maintain control and despite the loss of two engines flew the aircraft back over the coast with the intention of baling the crew out. However one man discovered his parachute had been ripped by shell splinters and was not safe to use, so Carswell decided to try and reach an airfield and attempt a landing. Little progress had been made when another engine began to falter and Carswell ordered those with parachutes to leave while he kept control and tried to bring the bomber down. Unfortunately it was mountainous terrain and Carswell and the remaining crewman were killed in the crash.

The British Commonwealth's highest decoration for valour, the Victoria Cross, was awarded to one member of a Liberator aircrew — and in unique circumstances. No 200 Squadron RAF, based in Gambia, despatched its first operational Liberator sortie on 11 August 1943 having recently converted from Hudsons. While on patrol the aircraft, piloted by a 29-year-old New Zealander, Flg Off Lloyd Trigg, was directed to a position where a flying boat had reported attacking a U-boat. When the Liberator failed to return a search was organised, during which a Liberator dinghy with survivors was sighted 240 miles south-east of Dakar. It was 24 hours before a naval vessel reached and retrieved the exhausted men who were not the crew of the missing Liberator but survivors of the *U-468* that it had sunk! One man was the U-boat captain who told how the Liberator had been set on fire by their flak while manoeuvring to attack, yet had continued the run to drop its depth charges before plunging into the sea near the stricken submarine. The few German survivors had managed to swim to an empty dinghy released from the Liberator. Solely on the evidence of the *U-468's* survivors a posthumous VC was later awarded to Trigg.

138
The Germans who survived from the U-boat sunk by Trigg's Liberator and whose reports led to the award of a posthumous VC. *British Official*

139
Hail Columbia crash landed in Cyprus following the Ploesti mission. *G. W. Underwood*

138

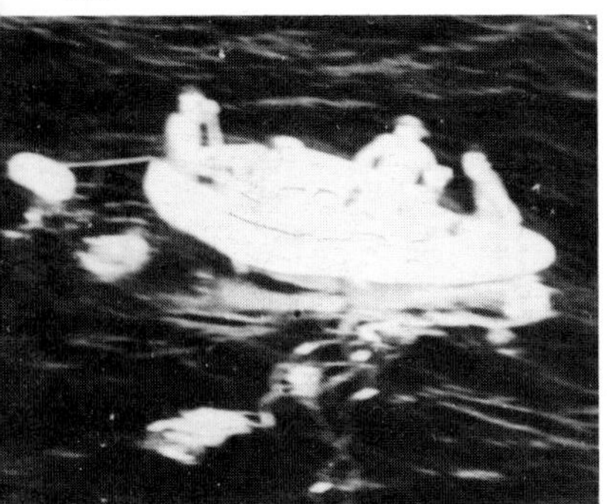

139

Medal of Honor Aircraft

Bruce A. Van Voorhis	PB4Y-1, 31992
Addison E. Baker	B-24D, 42-40994, D, *Hell's Wench*
John L. Jerstad	B-24D, 42-40994, D, *Hell's Wench*
Leon W. Johnson	B-24D, 41-23817, L, *Suzy Q*
John R. Kane	B-24D, 41-11825, V, *Hail Columbia*
Lloyd H. Hughes	B-24D, 42-40753, J
Leon R. Vance Jr	B-24H, 42-94830
Donald D. Pucket	B-24G, 42-78346
Horace S. Carswell Jr	B-24J, 44-40825

Victoria Cross Aircraft

Lloyd A. Trigg	Liberator V, BZ832, D

The Crew's Domain

Pilot

Art Cullen, 67th Bomb Squadron

'For its day the cockpit of the B-24 was spacious. The seating was good and fully adjustable so that most any pilot could get the comfortable position he required. We wore back-pack parachutes which formed the cushion of the seats on the B-24D. Controls and instruments were well placed and the three sets of four engine control levers — superchargers, throttles and mixture — on the pedestal were in easy reach of both pilot and co-pilot. The push-pull action on the control wheel worked the elevators and required only a little movement to have effect. Aileron response — through turning the wheel — was good. Rudder pedals were large and it didn't take long to discover why; an awful lot of pressure was required to shift those big twin rudders. The view from the cockpit was not as good as it could have been, particularly forward and down to the side. The sides of the cabin sloped inwards and to see down it was necessary to put your head against the side window or slide the plexiglass panel back. The cockpit noise was no higher than with other multi-engine airplanes of the day. In any case the dominant sound was the musical tones of the VHF radio coming through the headset. The B-24 was very nimble at medium altitudes: at high altitude it got very sloppy, more so when heavily loaded. I can best liken it to being on top a ball and socket; you could slide off any way. When levelling off after a high altitude climb the B-24 would tend to have a nose-up sit. If possible we would continue the climb a couple of hundred feet higher than the desired altitude and then descend to that level to pick up speed and get the nose down. The B-24 seemed a more flimsy aircraft than the B-17 and the wings would noticeably flex up and down. I think it was just as tough and being a more modern design than the B-17 it had flexibility built into it.'

140

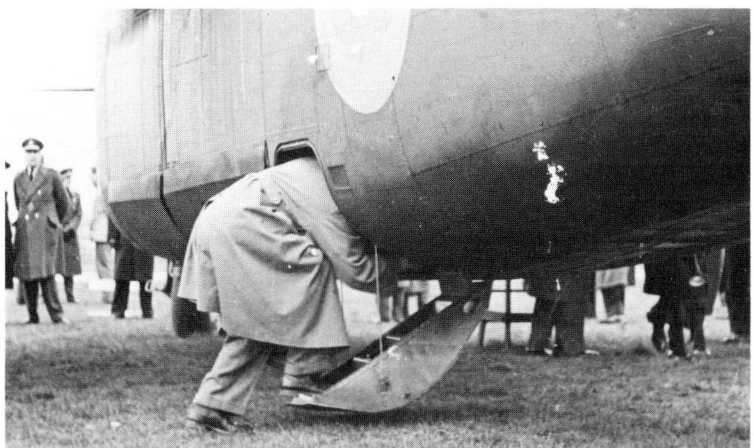

141

142

140
The Liberator I and B-24A had a swing step door on the lower left fuselage just aft of the bomb-bay. *IWM*

141/142
Later Liberators could be entered from the 18in wide nose wheel hatch, but that meant an awkward crawl through the passage under the flight deck.

143
To reach the flight deck it was easier to duck under the bomb-bay and squeeze by its passengers — if there was room. When empty this was always the way in and out for pilots.

144
Gunners could use the under-hatch but it was a long and awkward haul for anyone having to go through to the flight deck.

145
The hatch door was hinged and last man in closed and secured it.

146
The interior of Liberators differed depending on model and mission. Unless otherwise stated the following sequence depicts a Pathfinder B-24L. From the hatch a walkway ran to the rear turret, with an ammunition feed on one side and the chemical toilet on the other.

147
The tail gunner did not enter the turret until the aircraft was airborne and he was not supposed to land in it. If he did he was liable to be pitched into the gun sight when the main wheels impacted. A back-pack parachute could be worn in the turret by a slim man but it was a tight squeeze. Most gunners kept their 'chutes on the step just outside the doors.

148
Ingress and exit were always difficult when wearing heavy clothing.

143

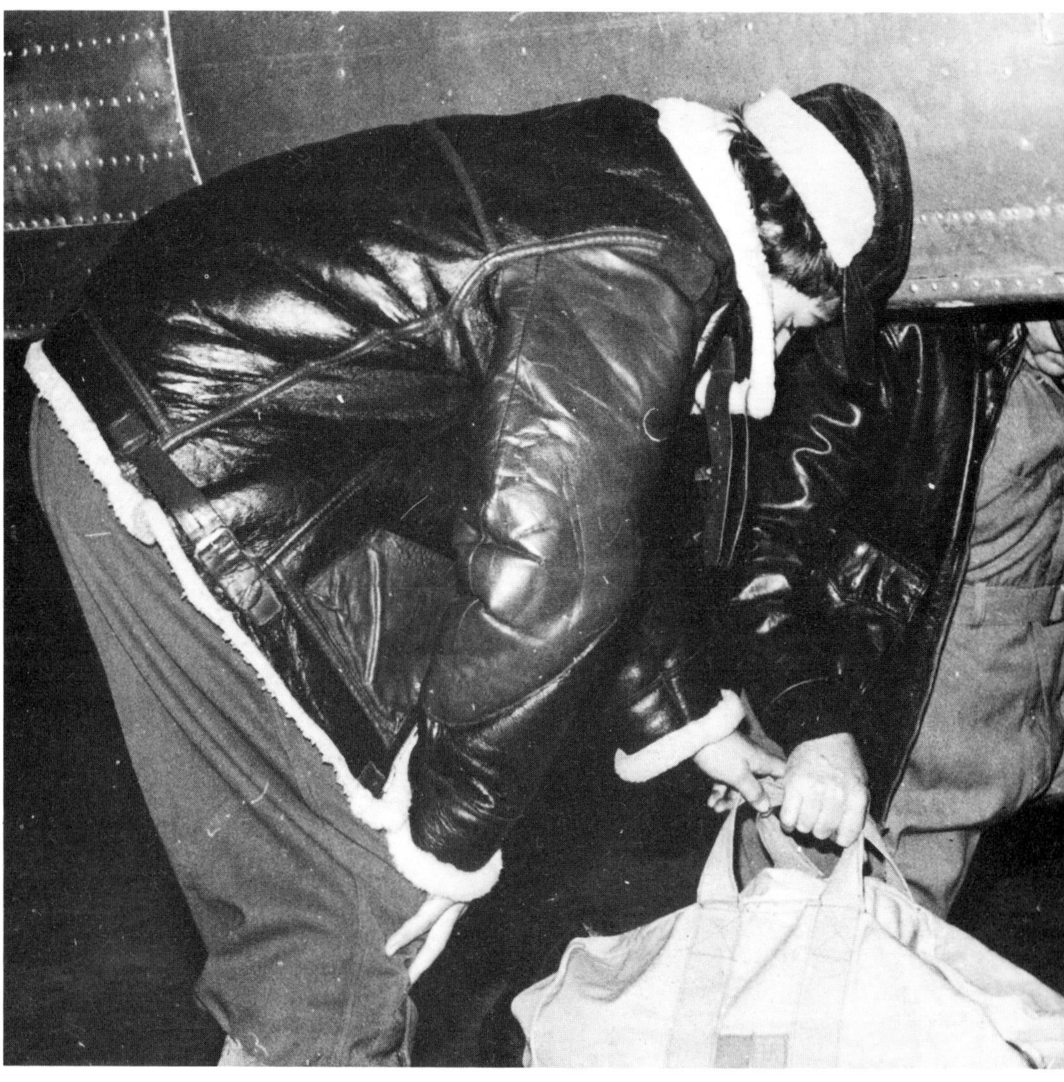

144

145

146

Tail Gunner

Paul Barr, 436th Bomb Squadron

'The B-24 tail gun position was better than the B-17's on which I did most of my training. I always felt more remote from the crew in a B-17 whereas in a '24 the waist gunners were in full view if the turret doors were open — and I liked to fly with them open. The Consolidated turret was a sturdy mount for the guns and I could shoot more accurately with it than the power-boost stinger turret fitted to a few of the later B-24s we received. The stinger turret was less cluttered and gave better visibility but I felt happier in the Consolidated as there was more protection for the gunner. Riding the tail in any bomber can be a rough ride and the B-24 was no exception. I never took off or landed in the turret as the whip and acceleration could throw your head on to the gun sight. As the plane I flew most of my tour in had enclosed waist windows the only time I got an air blast in the back of the turret was when the bomb doors were opened. Depending on the altitude we were flying it could be a cold place. The only Jap fighter that ever came near our plane came in on the tail. I got in a one second burst; didn't hit him; he was there and gone before I had time to track him. If he fired at us he didn't hit either.'

147

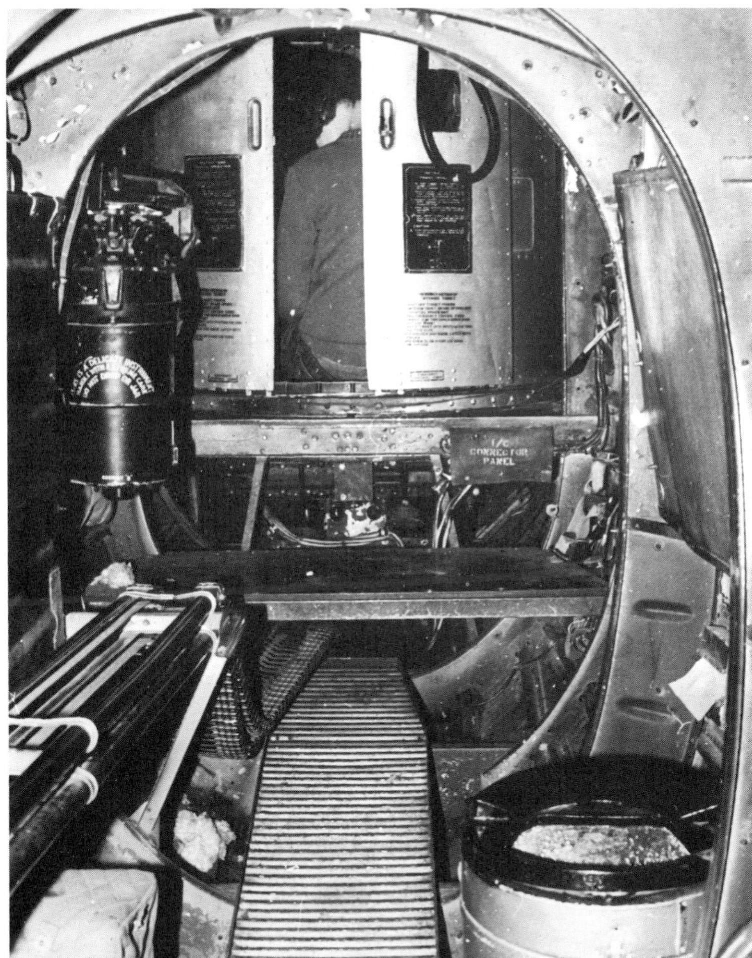

148

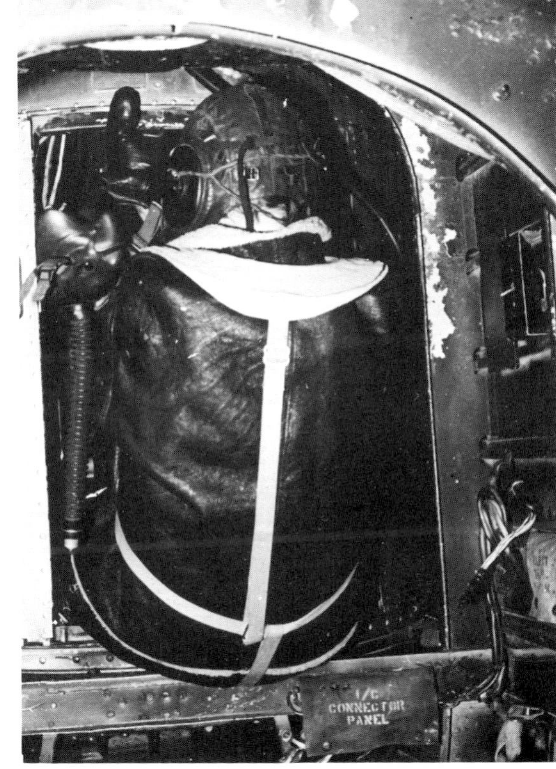

149
Waist window covers folded up inside the fuselage on early models. The waist was a good vantage point for observations, these crewmen being assigned to a PB4Y-1 of VB-103 in 1943.

150
In the Liberator I and B-24A the waist windows were higher than on later models as the internal structure of the fuselage was different. The huge fins and rudders limited field of fire to the rear. This gunner is S/Sgt James G. Osborne, who also acted as assistant flight engineer.

151
On the Liberator Mk II, III and V the RAF often installed twin .303in calibre machine guns in one half of the waist window allowing the gunner to sight through the other side. *IWM*

152
Wind deflectors could be opened in flight to dissipate slip stream entering the waist windows.

149

150

151

152

Waist Gunner

Bill Robertie, 68th Bomb Squadron

'There were good and bad things about being a waist gunner in a B-24. The good things were that you could move around and weren't cramped up like the turret gunners; you had a better view of the outside world than anyone else in the plane; and with those big waist windows and the nearby floor hatch you had a better change of escape if it ever came to baling out in a hurry. The bad things were having to stand over your gun for hours; the cold and breeze; and being bucked around by any sudden changes in flight attitude the pilots made.

'There was a slipstream deflector at the forward end of each waist window which could be swung out to keep out the worst of the blast but it was still pretty breezy at the gun.

'The point-fifty wasn't difficult to manipulate but the kick made accurate aim difficult. If I'm honest I'd say that you just pointed the gun in the direction of the target and hoped. Any enemy planes shot down by waist gunners were more by luck than skill and I think most men would go along with that.'

Ball Turret Gunner

Ed Smith, 514th Bomb Squadron

'The ball turret was no place for a nervous guy. Stuck down there under the belly of the B-24 it was too easy to worry about what would happen if things went wrong. There were stories about the turret mechanism jamming, the retraction gear failing, being isolated by a fire in the fuselage and the turret dropping off. I guess they happened only I never saw anything like that. My greatest fear was if something happened on the ship I wouldn't have time to get back up and get my 'chute on. The ball had an electric/hydraulic retraction mechanism which brought it way up into the fuselage until only the ends of the gun barrels stuck out below the fuselage. It had to be that way when lowered so that the hatches could be opened to allow entry. The general rule was for the ball to be lowered when we started over enemy territory. It was reckoned to take 10-15mph off our speed so the pilot didn't have it down any longer than necessary. While they didn't pick big fellows to ride the ball, I'm no small man and I could fit with fair comfort. It was no place to be for a long time as there wasn't a mite of room to stretch. You prayed the electric heating in your suit didn't go out because it could quickly become an icebox. And curled up there looking between your legs you soon wanted to move. The worst problem was urinating; I had my own set-up for getting around the problem. The view from the ball was certainly sensational; there's nothing more humbling than to realise that all there is between you and a five mile drop to earth is a canvas safety strap and a glass panel. The guns and feed only allowed good vision straight ahead so to search the turret had to be continully revolved. Fact, to pick up an enemy coming in you needed a warning of his approach if you were to stand a chance of hitting it. The only time I was able to get fighters in my sight was in tail attacks as they dived away under our ship. When you fired you'd think the ball was going to rip right outa the ship. The thing I hated most was going into a flak cloud. I'd bring the guns up to the horizontal so the armoured door at the back was facing to the ground. I'd swing the ball so I faced the tail going into flak and swing round to the front as we went out of it. It may not have made things safer but this way I didn't get to see how close it was coming!'

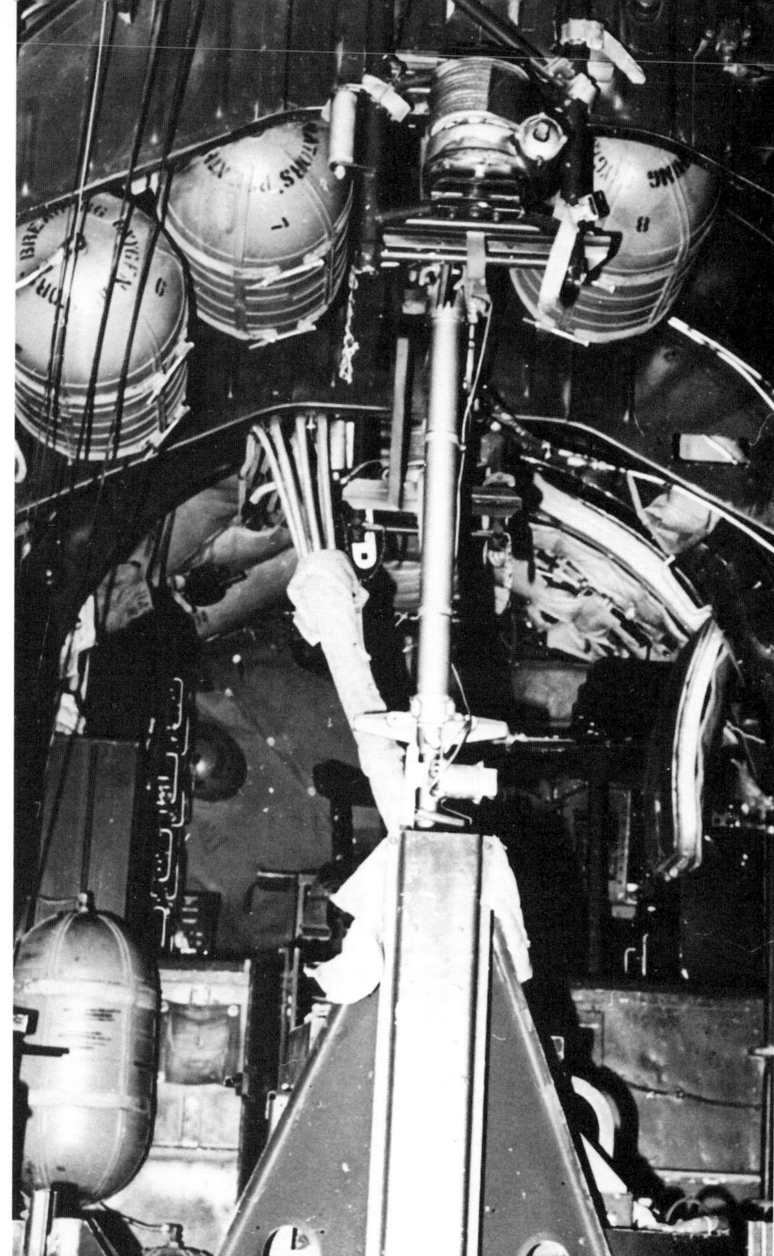

153

154

155

153
Forward from the waist gun area was the ball turret or radome gimbal and retraction unit, in this case a radome. Cables lead from scanner to instruments.

154
On operations the gunner entered the ball turret from inside the aircraft when it was lowered for action. It was possible to enter from the ground to carry out maintenance. *IWM*

155
Crew oxygen bottles were normally located above the rear bomb-bay, aft of the fuel tanks but in this B-24L Pathfinder they have been relocated in the rear fuselage and the original area used for resiting the radio operator. Below the radio operator's position can be seen the entrance to the bomb-bay.

156
In RAF Liberator Is used by the Return Ferry Service back-to-back passenger seating was installed above the rear bomb-bay. It was all rather spartan. These aircraft did not have the external life raft ejection hatches of later Liberators, hence the large inflatable dinghy slung in the fuselage. *Flight*

157
Entry point into the bomb-bay from the rear fuselage. In the foreground is the flexible conduit for radar cables.

156

157

Radio Operator
Ted Hine, 356 Squadron

'The Liberator VIs (B-24J) I flew in had the radio operator's equipment on the flight deck directly behind the pilot. I sat at a small metal table which had the receiver on top and the transmitter underneath. The position was cramped but not unduly so. The seat was a simple backless stool, not very comfortable for long flights but one got used to it. The flexes to my earphones were sufficiently long to allow me to stand up and look into the cockpit during take-offs and landings and at other times I could also act as another pair of eyes for the pilots and gunners. The only time I would leave my radio during a flight was when I had to go back to the rear of the aircraft to answer the call of nature. Apart from being able to look up ahead through the cockpit perspex I also had a small observation window in the fuselage side against my radio. There was always plenty of radio noise, particularly W/T (morse) but I never tuned in deliberately to the various American radio programmes that could be picked up at random. That way you could fail to receive important messages affecting the whole outcome of an operation.

'On long flights the radio operator's lot could be monotonous but one did have other members of the crew close at hand and knew just what was going on by way of the intercom and visual observation.'

158

159

160

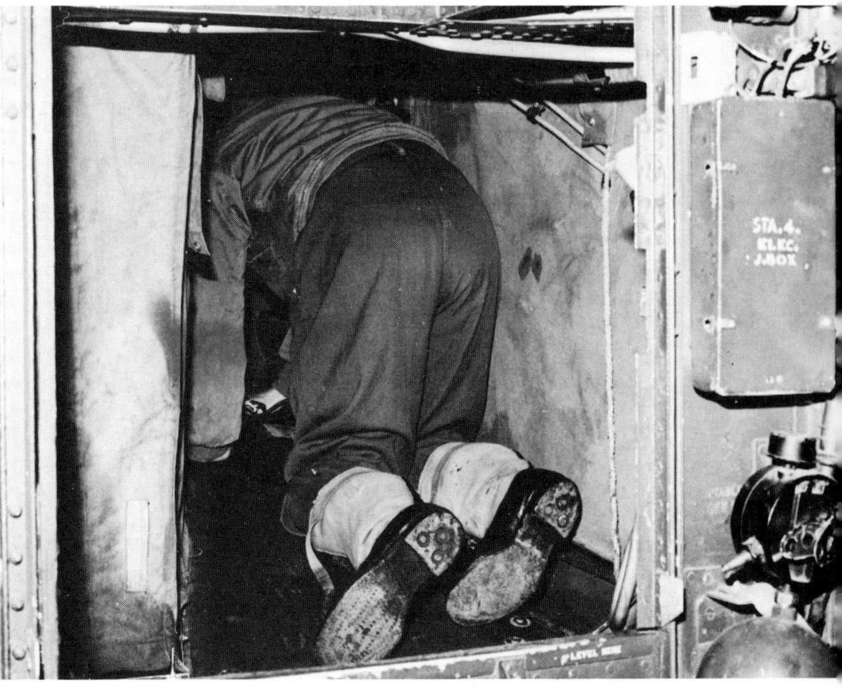

161

158
The bomb-bay walkway was 10in wide. As the upright beams forming the bomb-racks splayed out a little there was 14in higher up, but still no place for a big man to pass.

159
The all-essential relief tube was situated at the front end of the bomb-bay walkway.

160
At the end of the bomb-bay walkway were two hatches, one above the other. The lower hatch was the entrance to a 7ft tunnel leading round the nose wheel into the bombardier and navigator's compartment.

161
Pulling down a small step ladder over the lower opening allowed access to the flight deck.

162
Ahead lay the radar operator's position on the left, engineer's seat on the right and the cockpit beyond these. The top turret was also entered from this area. This is the layout on a B-24L pathfinder. Generally the radio operator was located on the right and the engineer on the left.

162

163
The radar navigator sat behind the pilot's bulkhead facing the rear to monitor his instruments.

164
In the B-24A and early Liberators the Flight Engineer occupied the right side of the aircraft. Here T/Sgt Joe Benkovic watches his gauges which are, from top to bottom: display generator charge, oil pressure, oil temperature, carburettor air temperature, cylinder head temperature, engine RPM and manifold pressure for each engine. On later models most of this instrumentation was moved into the cockpit.

165
The cockpit pedestal was surmounted by throttle levers and engine controls. The large round disc is the aileron tab control. To its immediate left is the flap lever and on its right the landing gear lever. Rudder trim tab knob is directly above the aileron tab control.

166
Looking in the pilot's window at cockpit controls and instrumentation. Back and forth movement of the control wheel operated elevators and wheel movement the ailerons.

166

167

167
The engines hid the wing tip from the pilots' view. It could present a problem in ground manoeuvres, particularly when close to buildings.

168
Due to inward sloping side windows, pilots sat low and their view over the nose was poor.

169
Patrol Plane Commander Gus Binnebose of VB-103 and his co-pilot, Lt Chandler in a PB4Y-1. It was common practice for pilot and co-pilot to have earphones lifted from one ear to allow direct shouted communication rather than using the interphone (the US Navy originally employed hand instead of throat microphones). In later years some former Liberator pilots tended to be hard of hearing in the right ear and co-pilots in the left!

170
Forward end of the tunnel from nose to bomb-bay. No place through which to make a hurried exit.

171
Looking forward from the entrance tunnel towards the bombardier's panel and his floor position for operating the bomb sight. Above are the front turret entrance doors.

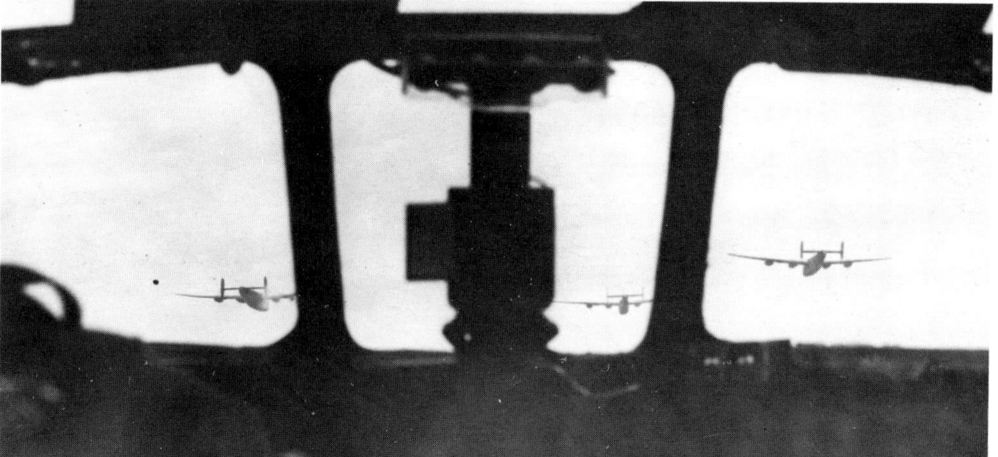
168

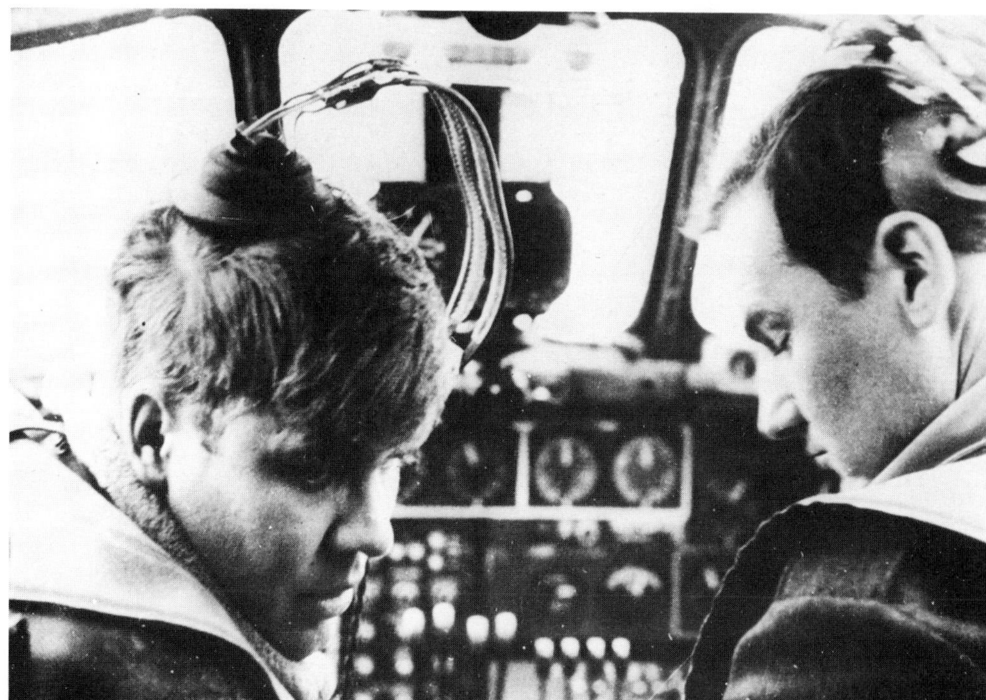
169

170

171

Bombardier

Charles Freudenthal, 489th Bomb Group

'The bombardier's station in a B-24 — the models with a nose turret — was pretty tight. With flak suits, parachutes, steel helmets and other equipment and the navigator you could get tangled up nearly every time you moved. It was far from the ideal workplace for setting up a run on a target. The nose turret made it necessary for the bombardier to crouch way down to operate the Norden sight. He normally knelt on his right knee. Since all knobs of the Norden sight were on the right side, he would reach across with the left hand to operate the "Turn and Drift" knob (deflection). The right hand operated the "Mirror drive clutch" (rate knob), which determined whether you were over, short, or on target. In this position the view down and directly ahead through the plexiglass was sufficient for the task, once the plane was lined up for the target, but there were nowhere near enough windows to allow for scanning. Finding the target was always the problem and even when visibility was good both bombardier and navigator had to work hard pinpointing to ensure a successful approach. As I usually flew lead the problem of watching for the release of bombs by other planes in the formation didn't often arise. For bombardiers who were toggling (releasing their bombs on sight of the lead's drop) the fact that the nose turret obscured vision above the horizontal plane was a headache. Toggling bombardiers would ride the nose turret when not at their sight. Usually a lead crew would have a "pilotage" navigator in the nose turret. Concentrating on setting up the run you'd forget the man in the turret and if he fired a burst, being just above your head, it really made you jump. The seal round the front turret never seemed to be effective and an icy draught was nearly always present, although this troubled the navigator most. Actually, the biggest discomfort I personally found was that in the first electrically heated flying suits we had — the one piece "long john" types, it could get very warm behind one's knee's when kneeling or sitting, since the wiring seemed to bunch up.'

172

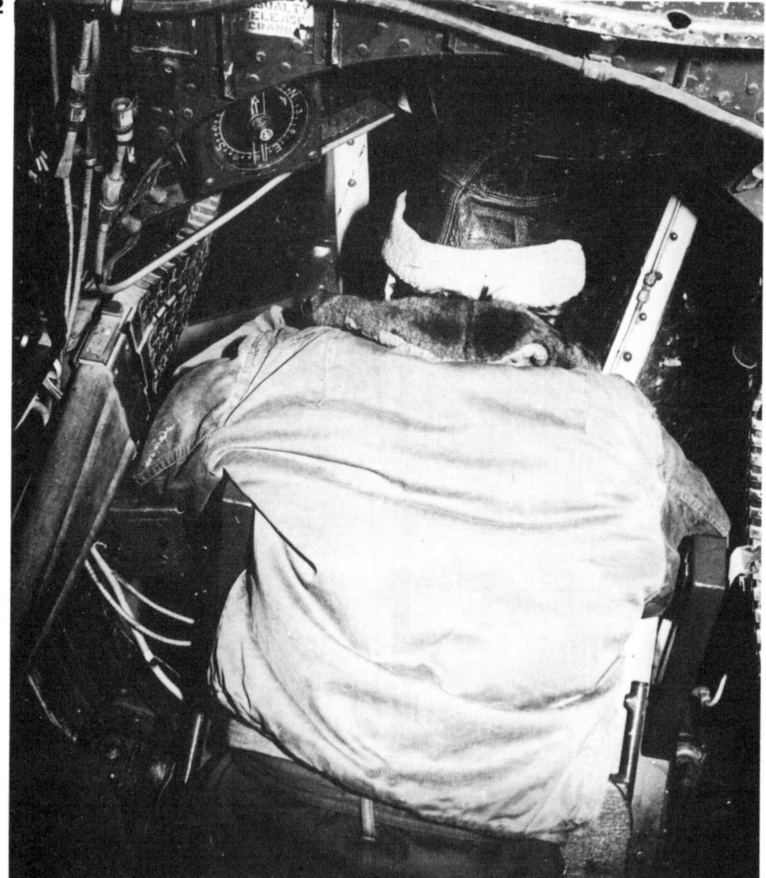

173

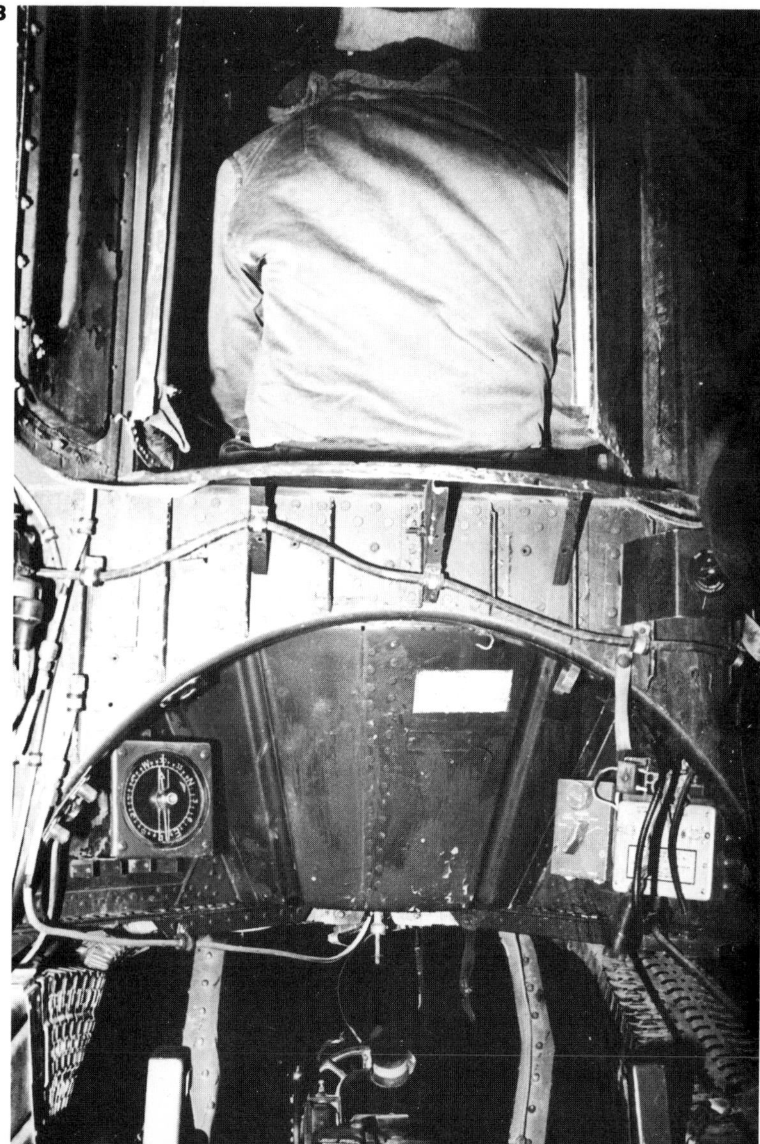

Navigator

Delmer Wangsvick, 732nd Bomb Squadron

'I always think they almost forgot the navigator when they developed the B-24 and then slotted him in between the bombardier and the nose wheel. A navigator has maps, papers and needs plenty of space to work. In the B-24 he got a narrow table fixed to the nose compartment bulkhead where he sat on a skimpy seat facing the pilots' feet and plumb in the way of the bombardier or nose gunner whenever they went back to the flight deck. There was always enough air whipping in around the sides of that darn nose turret to make it necessary to pin down any papers or they'd be blown way back to the bomb bay. A single bulged observation window on either side of the nose provided the only places the navigator could look out to make ground checks. These windows were far too small and because visibility was so limited the navigator's job was made harder. In visual conditions he was back and forth to the side windows craning his neck for most of the mission. A lot is said about B-24 pilots having a heavy time on the controls and being mighty tired after a mission but I can tell you a navigator was just as ready for the sack. For take-offs and landings I went back to the flight deck and sat near the liaison transmitter. This was for safety in case the nose wheel collapsed. The nose was no place to be in a crack-up. Although the compartment was a cold, shaky place my only real complaint about the navigator's position was the poor look out.

'I did at times get a change when I flew the "Command Navigator" position. As such, I did no "commanding" but operated the nose turret and assisted the crew navigator, primarily in picking out visual checkpoints and occasionally making recommendations to the pilot. A different matter of concern in this position was the possibility of having trouble in making a hurried exit in case the turret got stuck on "Azimuth" for some reason or other. Otherwise — provided there were no enemy fighters — this position could be almost pleasant and relaxing.'

174

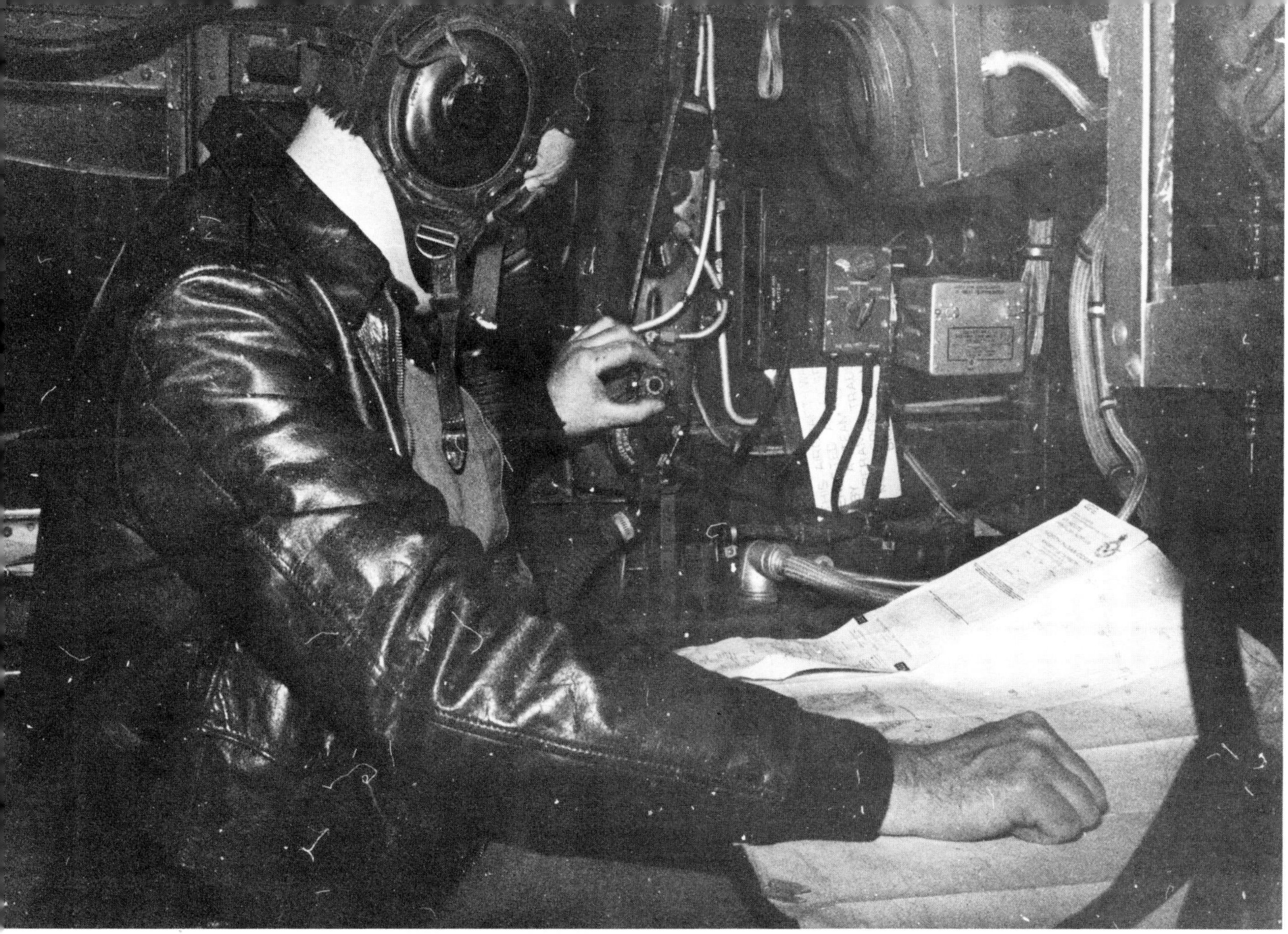

172
Bombardier in position at his sight.

173
Bombardier in the nose turret. Bombsight visible below.

174
Navigator sat at a small table on the left side of nose in very cramped quarters.

175
From the flight deck it was possible to see the navigator through the cables, pipes and control chains under the instrument panel.

175

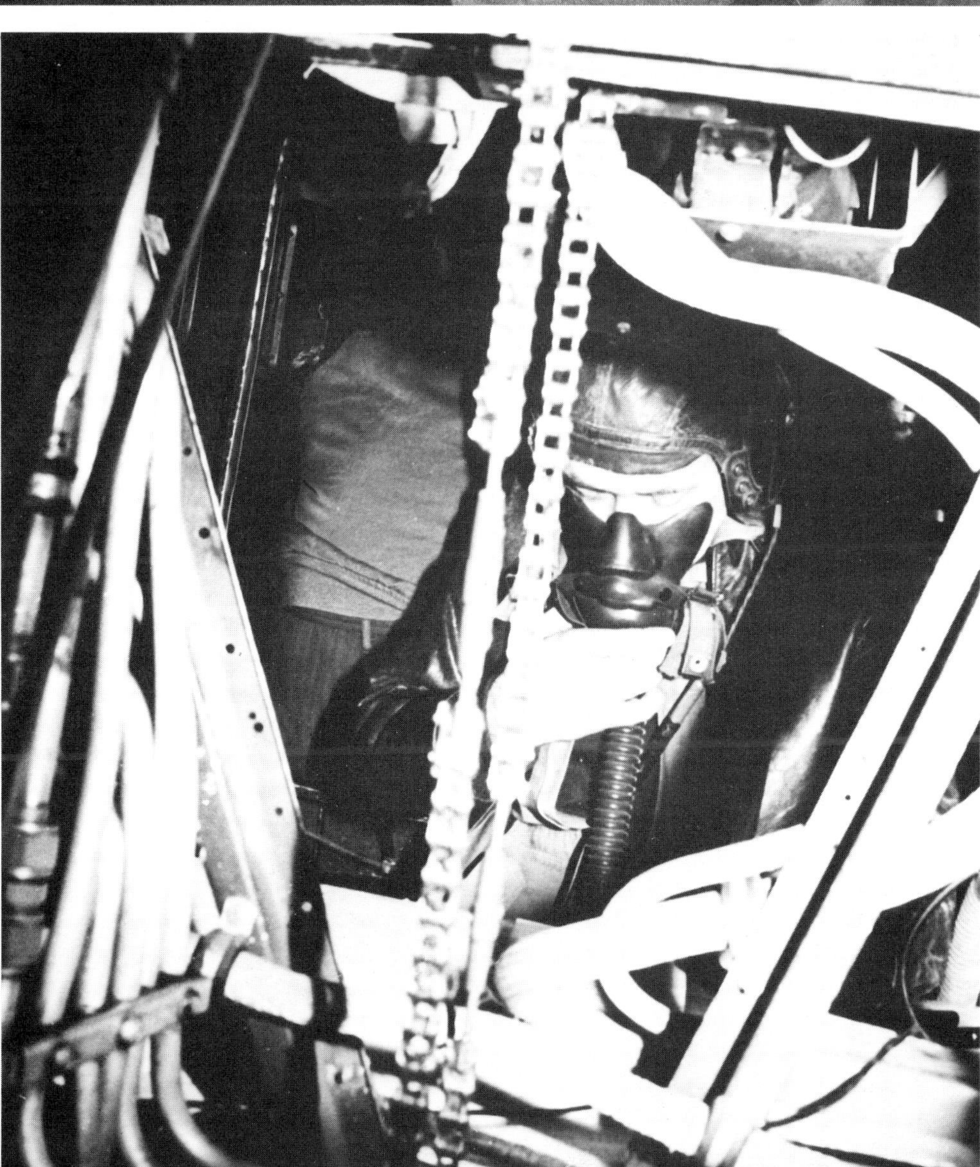

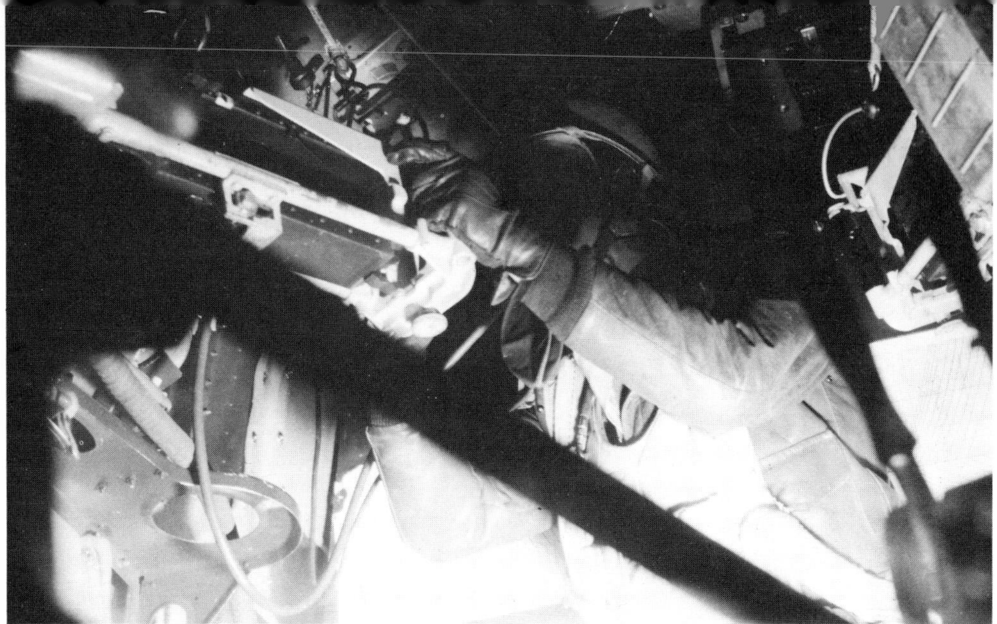

176
In the B-24D the bombardier manned the hand-held nose guns. There was little room for manoeuvre.
via J. Archer

177
The early Liberators provided a much better outlook from the nose. Flt Sgt Bert Coates was navigator and bomb aimer on a Liberator II.

Top-Turret

Ted Parker, 855th Bomb Squadron

'The top-turret gunner was usually also the flight engineer. When out of the turret he sat on a jump seat on the right side of the flight deck and monitored the fuel gauges and operated the transfer system. He also checked on the engines and generators during the early stage of a mission. As the ball turret wasn't used in our group, there was some rearrangement of gunners, and I flew the top turret so the engineer was free for his duties. It was usual to climb up into the Martin turret once over the sea and fire a test burst. The gunner's head was low in the turret so you didn't have much of a view below the horizontal and parts of the turret mechanism blocked your view at that level on both sides. Apart from that there was excellent visibility as the plexiglass was frameless. I found the seat and foot rest gave a fairly easy position and from the point of view of gunner comfort it was the best defence position to fly on a B-24. The sun on the curves of plexiglass made glare that could be a nuisance even with tinted glasses. Constantly swinging the turret around with the sun beating down could make you drowsy after a few hours and it became difficult to stay keyed up for a possible fighter attack. With the guns so close to your head the noise and kick when they were fired was terrific. Smoke tended to stay in the top of the turret and could be troublesome. It was important that the bomb-bay hatch was closed when firing to prevent spent links and cases falling down and jamming the bomb-bay doors. The Martin Turret generally had no problems, was easy to operate and a pretty effective defence point.'

A Fearsome Beast

The warrior's adornment of his equipment with ferocious beasts dates from the dawn of military history. Warships of the ancients were notable for prows shaped and painted to represent the heads of fearsome creatures with the purpose of frightening an enemy. The snarling tooth-lined mouths decorating the noses of World War 2 aircraft were part fancy decoration, part symbol of defiance, and more likely to amuse the foe than terrify him. The type of nose that invited such artistry was usually that with a deep air scoop below a propeller spinner, the intake becoming the mouth. Like most multi-engine bombers, the early Liberators with their 'glasshouse' noses were quite unsuitable but with the introduction of a front turret, the type's forward fuselage took on an uncanny resemblance to a face. The turret became a nose, the bombardier's window an open mouth and the navigator's side observation windows eyes. This potential was soon noticed by operational units and taken advantage of. In fact, such was the extent of beast faces on Liberators it seems probable that at some stage or another every USAAF B-24 group featured such a decoration on one of its aircraft. Some beast noses represented specific creatures — dogs, dragons, whales, sharks, etc — but mostly the face was just an awesome monster. One early B-24J operated by a training unit in the United States had a particularly colourful and elaborate beast nose modelled on a lion. A colour photograph of this artwork was reproduced in a wartime aviation magazine and immediately became a model for similar paint schemes applied to B-24s overseas. The 8th Air Force had at least five examples based on this particular scheme. In some cases beast noses became unofficial squadron or group markings and when this happened a simple stylised design was adopted.

178

178
Although not the first Liberator to be decorated with a row of teeth around the lower part of the nose, the decorations on this aircraft did perpetuate a whole series of imitations. An Oklahoma City Modification Center turret graft and nose rebuild brought permission to paint this particular job to represent a beast face. The resulting lion-like artwork attracted a photographer and eventually a full page colour spread depicting this aircraft appeared in a magazine.

179
The 389th Bomb Group made a fairly worthy copy on a B-24H.

180
The 458th Bomb Group introduced variations when they decorated 42-100408, a B-24J, in this style. *via M. Bailey*

181
The RCAF's No 10 Squadron at Gander also took a fancy to this artwork and Liberator GR VI 3742 soon bore another representation. *via Leo Blum*

182
There were a great many simpler forms of beast nose. This 11th Bomb Group B-24D was extra ferocious, the jaws incorporating the whole turret. *via M. Bailey*

183
Tubarao of the 491st BG featured a curling tongue. *via M. Bailey*

184
The Gremlin's Roost of 392nd Bomb Group appeared almost jolly.

179

180

181

182

183

184

185

186

187

185
And 458th Bomb Group's *Flak Magnet* quite definitely had a grin.

186
While on 453rd Bomb Group's *Little Joe* it was no more than a stylised decoration.

187
With the CBI based 308th Bomb Group towards the end of hostilities a 'shark nose' became an unofficial insignia carried by most aircraft. The mouth always had a downwards twist, giving a rather mean look. *via M. Bailey*

188
Another 308th Bomb Group shark nose (42-73438 of 374th Bomb Sqn) in white, red and black with a blue 'eye'. *A. Ondris*

189
In 93rd Bomb Group's 330th Bomb Squadron the decoration was adopted to represent the unit's whale insignia. Most aircraft came to sport whale noses like that on *Solid Comfort*. *via M. Bailey*

188

189

Up For A World Turn

Range became a major consideration in the planning and execution of air operations during the truly global World War 2. It was of paramount importance in the war with Japan where vast areas of water had often to be bridged in offensive action against the enemy. The Liberator, with its generous tankage and good endurance, was from the early days of hostilities recognised as having the best range for heavy bombing operations in the Pacific and South-East Asia war zones and, by the late summer of 1944, was the most numerous of all Allied aircraft on the scene.

In eastern India and Ceylon, where there was a sizeable force of American and British Liberators conducting operations against the Japanese in Burma and Malaya, RAF units were increasingly required to attack targets across the Bay of Bengal entailing round trips of over 2,500 miles. Fuel conservation was essential on such sorties, particularly with the new and heavier Liberator VI (B-24J). Moreover, as received from the United States the new model Liberators were found to have endurance limitations that restricted an operational bomb load to 4,000lb for a round trip of 1,200 miles. As this fell well below what was required in the theatre the CO of the RAF's oldest Liberator bomber unit, No 159 Squadron, Wg Cdr James Blackburn, on his own initiative began a programme of experimentation aimed at improving the payload and range of the Liberator.

Blackburn began by purging the Liberator of equipment non-essential to the type of operations being flown, which included some armament and the oxygen system. As RAF bomber missions were usually conducted at an optimum 8,000ft, deletion of the turbo-superchargers, which totalled some 1,500lb, was considered but the engineering involved was too complicated. The wing commander then began a laborious session of test flights, experimenting with power settings to obtain minimum fuel burn-off for a given load. Eventually he established a combination of mixture, propeller speed and throttle settings which, plus a few degrees of flap, allowed the aircraft to mush along at 160mph air speed but produced a range of 3,000 miles. With the addition of forward bomb-bay fuel tanks the potential was as great as 4,000 miles. All this was achieved at around 8,000ft with an aircraft originally developed to give optimum performance at 25,000ft. Sceptical of these claims, a manufacturers' representative came to see and it took a demonstration flight to convince him.

Operational application of Blackburn's findings allowed No 159 Squadron to mine Penang harbour on 26 October 1944, taking 18hr to make the 3,000-mile flight there and

190
BZ826, one of the aircraft that was used on the first mining operation to Singapore on 26/27 March 1945. The Liberator V previously served with 200 Squadron at Madras.
John Griffin

190

191
KH391 which set a combat endurance record for late model Liberators on 26/27 March 1945 when flown by Sqn Ldr Tommy Lee and crew of 357 Squadron. The aircraft, a Mk VI, was transferred to the Indian Air Force in the immediate postwar years and served with No 6 Squadron at Poona/Lohgaon airfield. It was photographed there in February 1969. *Steve Simm*

192
The Liberator that stayed up for a world turn. BZ862 in which Flt Lt Jack Muir and crew flew what is believed to be the longest combat operation performed by any landplane during World War 2. This photograph was taken when BZ862 was serving with 354 Squadron. *K. O. Phillips*

192

back to its Indian base. On other occasions the technique allowed RAF Liberators to convey 10,000lb bomb loads on five-hour sorties. Other squadrons were to squeeze even greater endurance out of the Liberator, most notably No 160, the maritime reconnaissance unit based in Ceylon.

By 1945 No 160 was gradually extending its mining operations — that came to be known as 'Nutting' sorties — southwards along the Malayan coast. There remained one particular goal, Singapore. Although some 1,600 miles from No 160's base, the mining of Singapore harbour could cause considerable disruption to Japanese shipping. The CO, Wg Cdr John Stacey, was busy exploiting the fuel conserving techniques Blackburn had pioneered and found that they were particularly advantageous when applied to the Liberator V, the maritime version of the B-24D which the squadron preferred. The Mk V was lighter, speedier and consequently handled better than later marks, and because of this 160 had made efforts to retain them. Now Stacey planned to use them to reach Singapore and having received Command sanctions readied eight for the task. Top turrets were removed and all equipment not essential to the mission — even the chemical toilet was not sacrosanct. Each aircraft carried 3,280 US gallons of fuel, 400 of which was in two forward bomb-bay tanks, and 75 in a Catalina overload tank slung above them, while the rear bay held three 1,000lb magnetic mines.

The mission was despatched during the

afternoon of 26 March. Weather could hardly have been worse as vast storm clouds rising to more than 20,000ft covered much of the Bay of Bengal. Flying just below the cloud base and a few hundred feet above the ocean, rain and gales slowed progress to a point where the force was an hour late on its flight plan when only half-way to the target. The weather cleared for the run into the target area and seven of the Liberators deposited their mines in the Johore Strait separating Malaya from Singapore. The eighth aircraft had so diminished its fuel in battling through the storm that the pilot was forced to abandon the attempt to reach Singapore and instead unloaded over a secondary target area. Storms had to be penetrated on the return flight but all Liberators returned safely to base. The average flight time was 21hr 30min for the round trip of 3,460 miles with one aircraft taking 22hr 6min. Approximately 17hr of the flight had been through rain and clouds on which Stacey commented, 'I have never seen so much lightning in my life'. However, on the same night Liberator VI, KH391 of No 357 Squadron, piloted by Sqn Ldr Tom Lee had carried out a supply drop deep in enemy held southern Malaya which was of an astonishing 22hr 45min duration. No 357 Squadron specialised in such delivery operations to organised behind-the-lines resistance in Burma, Malaya and Indo-China. Using stripped down Mk VIs with extra bomb-bay fuel tanks many of its operations exceeded 20hr in the air.

Nearly a month after its first visit to Singapore, No 160 Squadron returned on another 'Nutting' mission. Seven aircraft were despatched on 24 April and when they returned next day, BZ830 'T' piloted by Flt Lt Percy Waddy had strafed a Japanese trawler, evaded ack-ack and fighters, covered 3,520 miles and been in the air 22hr 10min. (Waddy, like many of the pilots in No 160, was a Canadian.) The waters around Singapore were again replenished with Mk 36 mines on the night of 30-31 May by four Liberator Vcs and again new duration records were established for the Squadron with Flt Lt Roy Schroeder's crew in BZ867 'P' making 22hr 22min and Flt Lt Leo Davidson in FL991 'F' close behind with 22hr 18min. Each aircraft delivered three mines. These sorties were flown at 1,000ft and down to 500ft when in range of enemy radar.

In June 1945 No 160 Squadron also became involved in the 'special delivery' business. Twenty hour sorties became almost commonplace and more records were in the offing. Flying a clandestine sortie code named Carpenter 30 on the night of 20 July, Flt Lt V. T. Davis and crew in BZ862 'J' touched down at Minneriya, Ceylon, 22hr 51min after leaving. After such flights there were often several hundred gallons of fuel remaining in the tanks and it seemed possible that someone in the squadron would soon pass the 23-hour mark. It happened on the night of 29 July when two aircraft were sent to a dropping zone near Sedili Besar in Malaya to parachute supplies in the moonlight. Flg Off L. W. Millard in BZ862 'J' returned to base 23hr 3min after take-off while Flg Off S. D. Turner in BZ824 'W' clocked up the extraordinary 23hr 23min. Many people believed that this was about the ultimate in endurance for a Liberator — if not for the eight- or nine-man crew who had to suffer the constant noise and vibration. Indeed, no one set out to establish endurance records; the reverse was the case as fatigue was such that nothing was spared to terminate a long range sortie as quickly as possible.

Two nights after the Sedili Besar operation the same two aircraft, which had shown good fuel conservation, were despatched on another special delivery, this time to a location near Kota Tinggi in south Malaya. Flt Lt Magnus's aircraft completed the sortie after 23hr 3min but Flt Lt J. A. Muir and his six-man crew were to experience difficulties resulting in a remarkable piece of Liberator history. Reaching the reception area none of the prearranged signal lights could be seen. Navigational checks were then carried out and these confirmed that the aircraft was at the correct location. Still with no signals from the ground and fuel reaching the level where only sufficient remained for the return trip, the 'load' — two British officers was dropped near the Kota Tinggi-Johore Bahru road. Jack Muir had then spent 85min flying in the vicinity of the drop zone. Liberator BZ862 'J' touched down at Minneriya at 0243hrs on 1 August 1945 having taken off at 0223hrs on 31 July and flown 3,735 statute miles. The aircraft had been airborne for 24hr 10min which was the longest combat sortie flown by a Liberator and, it is believed, also the longest made by an Allied land plane during World War 2.

193

193
Jack Muir, BZ862's pilot on the record flight of 31 July-1 August 1945. Following his service career Jack Muir joined Air Canada, retiring after more than 25,000 hours flying in their service. *J. Muir*

Remarkable Libs

194

194
USAAF's seventh Liberator (excluding prototypes), B-24A 40-2375, was one of two aircraft being prepared for a secret mission to photograph Japanese island bases when the attack on Pearl Harbor upset plans. This aircraft subsequently served with Ferry and Air Transport Commands, chiefly on the *Arnold Line* run across the North Atlantic to Prestwick, Scotland where it was photographed on 25 June 1942. It survived the war and went to the breakers with more than 10,000 flight hours on its airframe through plying the world's air routes. The ATC called it *Old Consistent*.

195

195
The fifth LB-30 Liberator II was AL507 which was commandeered by the USAAF in December 1941 and became *Dumbo I*, the first aircraft equipped with ASV Mk X, the new sea-scanning centermetric radar which was to prove a valuable aid in the war against the U-boats. AL507 flew to the UK in March 1942 and later underwent service tests. For a period it was flown by Sqn Ldr Bullock, the U-boat killing ace, with No 59 Squadron, and was photographed at Prestwick in that unit's markings.
Scottish Aviation

196
Because Liberator IIs had no turbo-superchargers many were modified for transport work. AL507's Coastal Command days being over it was flown to Canada and to Dorval underwent extensive modification receiving a new nose and even new spinners. *via J. Oughton*

197
AL507 ended her career on 2 October 1946 when the undercarriage was damaged during take-off from Prestwick for Gander. The captain — J. N. Wilson — flew around for ten hours burning off fuel and then made a gentle belly landing at Heathfield. The propellers did not even touch the ground. Sadly repair was not justified as there was a surplus of Liberator transports. *via J. Oughton*

198/199
Another Liberator II with varied service was AL552 which started out on anti-submarine patrols with No 160 Squadron from Northern Ireland then moved to the Middle East, flying more than 50 bombing sorties with No 178 Squadron. It too was transformed from a drab bomber into a shiny transport and went on to serve with European airlines in post-war years. When last heard of in the early 1950s it was still going strong with a French company. *via J. Oughton*

200
Many USAAF B-24s completed in excess of 100 bombing sorties, particularly creditable where the operating environment was unfavourable. One of the most remarkable records in Europe was that of 467th Bomb Group's *Witchcraft*, B-24H 42-52534, which flew 130 missions without ever once having to abandon a sortie through mechanical failure.

196

197

198

199

200

43-102

201
Not just another nice shiny Liberator B VI over England's south coast but a pioneer of automatic landing approaches. KL632 (44-49804) set off for the UK four days before VE Day but as the result of engine trouble did not leave North America until 10 months later having been diverted and used for the first installation of the Instrument Landing System (SCS-51) coupled with a Sperry auto-pilot. This Liberator was later used to prove that automatic landing approaches using commercial production equipment were a practical proposition, pioneering a system which was adopted and developed for airline use. Note antenna under nose.
via J. Oughton

201

The Famous

202
Liberators transported many famous people during the Second World War. Winston Churchill used AL504 *Commando* on flying visits to Allies and battle fronts. On this occasion the venue was Moscow. Molotov, Averell Harriman and the British Prime Minister stand beside the aircraft during the playing of their countries' anthems. Behind Molotov is Marshal Shaposhnikov, Soviet chief of General Staff. 12th August 1943. *IWM*

203
Commando and Churchill in the desert with Generals Alexander and Brook (on the PM's right) early 1943. *NAPS*

204
Princess Juliana of Holland made use of the rejuvenated *Commando* with a flight from Canada to London on 9 September 1944. She was met by her mother Queen Wilhelmina. *via J. Oughton*

205
Gulliver, 41-23863, was the first C-87A, a special VIP passenger transport with de luxe interior including 10 sleeping berths. Used by Wendell Willkie, the President's roving personal representative, it also made a little piece of history by giving the 22 year old Shah of Persia his first flight, a local joyride. This occurred when the aircraft made a stop-over at Tehran on 16 September 1942 during a 28,475 mile round-the-world trip visiting 17 countries. Man in the top hatch in this picture is wing tip watching; keeping lookout for obstructions the pilots cannot see. *IWM*

202

203

204

205

206

206
One of the most famous names associated with the B-24 in combat was film star James Stewart. He came to England in November 1943 with the 445th Bomb Group, commanded a squadron and in the following spring moved to the 453rd Bomb Group as Air Executive. On completion of his operational tour he served in the 2nd Bomb Wing headquarters until the end of hostilities. Although Stewart did his best to escape the film star tag, he was always accorded attention by photographers. This posed picture has Stewart in the centre of a group supposedly returning from an operational flight.

207
Liberator II, AL512, was connected with a different kind of fame. It was the aircraft on which Miss Elizabeth Drewry became the first female air stowaway to cross the Atlantic. She was found, very cold and cramped, in the nose wheel compartment when AL512 landed at Dorval, Canada on a regular Return Ferry Service flight from Prestwick on 20 November 1943. The 24-year old girl had previously worked for Scottish Aviation but was keen to secure a flying job and stowed away to Canada believing her chances of achieving this would be better in North America.

208
AM261 was the first Liberator to carry royalty when it conveyed the Duke of Kent (brother of the King) to Canada in 28 July 1941. Here the Duke enters the aircraft at Prestwick while VIPs see him off. This was also the first time any member of the British Royal family had flown the Atlantic. *IWM*

209
C-87A, *Guess Where II?* (41-24159) was prepared as Presidential transport. In the event the President never used the aircraft but his wife, Mrs Eleanor Roosevelt, did. The photograph was taken in Brazil when she was making a tour of Central and South America in May 1944. *via R. Mikesh*

207

208

209

Epilogue

A quarter of a century after the Liberator's brief monopoly of the sky, not more than could be counted on the fingers of two hands remained. Most of these reposed at Poona where the Indian Air Force had recently retired the last of a score of Liberator VIs inherited from the RAF in 1946. During the early-1970s a few aeronautical museums around the world, apprised of the dwindling numbers of this historical aircraft, managed to acquire the better examples of the Indian residue and fly them away into permanent preservation. In 1973 one such veteran Liberator reached England on route to the United States. The journey was broken at the Imperial War Museum's Duxford airfield where necessary repairs and overhaul were performed during the winter months in preparation for the long trans-Atlantic crossing the following year. Additionally, the aircraft was carefully repainted to represent a specific USAAF B-24 operated from England during World War 2.

It so happened that before the bomber's departure a sizeable party of American Liberator veterans and their families visited the Duxford museum. They were members of the Second Air Division Association, largest active B-24 veterans organisation, formed by those who served in England with the 8th Air Force's principal Liberator arm during the years 1942-1945. As a memorial to more than six thousand comrades lost in B-24s during hostilities, the men of the Division subscribed to the building of a special library room in Norwich, England, which they still maintain, stock with books and periodically visit as a group. It was during such an occasion that the visit to Duxford was arranged with the added appeal of an opportunity to inspect a B-24, an old friend which many of the veterans had not set eyes on for nearly 30 years.

The author was asked to act as one of the guides for the party who, despite the usual chill of an exposed airfield on an English

210
The Twecherous Wabbit goes to war. A B-24H of 487th Bomb Group lifts off a Lavenham runway on a blustery June day in 1944. Other Liberators on the skyline are marshalled to follow. *J. Archer*

May morn, found much of interest and appeared to enjoy the occasion. Understandably, to see and touch a B-24 again was an emotional experience for many men and certainly the high spot of the visit. There was also another attraction in the form of James Stewart, of Hollywood fame and himself a former England-based Liberator pilot, who had come to see the old bomber.

Parked on the concrete apron out in front of the hangars, the Liberator was not giant of the scene as it would once have been. Compared with more streamlined and meaningful looking warplanes parked nearby it seemed squat, ill contoured and utility. The uninitiated would have been unlikely to suspect that before them stood one of the great champions of air warfare.

When the veterans moved away to inspect other exhibits the guide noticed one man detach himself from the party and amble back across the apron towards the Liberator. He looked the archetype of what the British had come to think of as the typical middle-aged American tourist; smart raincoat, loud checkered pattern suit, colourful soft-brimmed hat over closely cropped hair and an array of camera equipment slung from one shoulder. Shortish, well rounded at the girth, thickening at neck and jowl, but the years had not masked facial features the guide had seen in many photographs taken near half a lifetime earlier. For this man was once a young, slim, tousle-haired officer who starred as a B-24 pilot, surviving more than 30 combat missions when only one in three did; who could count Ploesti, Kiel, Werner Neustadt and Berlin among targets and whose uniform carried ribbons that paid tribute to his bravery.

Thinking that the veteran might appreciate company in his further survey of the bomber and then direction to rejoin the rest of the party, the guide followed him across the apron. Later the guide was to reflect that he should have realised this man deliberately sought privacy by his action. On reaching the Liberator and dodging under the rear fuselage the guide saw the man standing beside the nose, slowly running a chubby hand over the shiny skin, much in the way one might caress a loved one. His eyes were filled with tears. The guide stopped, embarrassed, wishing to steal away unnoticed but the veteran was already aware of his presence. Keeping a hand pressed against the smooth metal he turned his head towards the guide, tears rolling down his cheeks and said with obvious feeling: 'They are for her. She did us proud; so very proud.'